The Forgotten Jesus

By Leo V. Cheeseman

Other books by Leo V. Cheeseman

The Heretic's Handbook – A Gameplan for Christian Growth

Scripture quotations are from the New Revised Standard Version of the Bible, copyright © 1989 National Council of the Churches of Christ in the USA. Used by permission. All rights reserved.

©2007 by Leo V. Cheeseman
ISBN 978-1-4303-2358-7

**All rights reserved by The Fellowship of LIGHT.
Published at Lulu.com/cheeseman**

for•get
verb transitive

2   : to treat with inattention or disregard <*forgot* their old friends>

3   : to disregard intentionally : OVERLOOK — usu. used in the imperative <*forget* it>

©1997, 1996 Zane Publishing, Inc. All rights reserved.

"The person who hears the teachings
Of Jesus and ignores or neglects them
Is worse off than the person
Who never hears them."
LVC

Luke 6: 46 "Why do you call me 'Lord, Lord,' and do not do what I tell you?"

James 1: 22 "But be doers of the word, and not merely hearers who deceive themselves."

Contents

Introduction	1
Faith	11
The Greatest Commandments	21
You Must Be Born Again	25
Witness	31
Temptations from Satan	37
Take up Your Cross	41
The Sermon on the Mount and Parallels	43
Beatitudes	43
The Law	47
Divorce and Adultery	51
Oaths	52
Behavior/Relationship	52
Prayer	56
The Lord's Prayer	56
Forgiveness	58
Fasting	59
Treasures on Earth	59
The Lamp of the Body	61
Two Masters	62
Depend on God	62
The Golden Rule	67
The Narrow Gate	69
The Saved and the Damned	70
Good Fruit/Bad Fruit	71
Other Forgotten Parables	75
Love, Trust and Obey God	76
Friend at midnight	78
Laborers in vineyard	78
Unjust judge	80
Two debtors	81
Two sons	81
Leavened bread	82
Wedding banquet	82
Love Your Neighbor	83

    Good Samaritan 84
    Great physician 85
    Unmerciful servant 86
Witness/Be fruitful 87
    Grain of wheat 88
    Barren fig tree 88
    Christian light 89
    Growing seed 90
    Householder 90
    The sower 91
    Vine and branches 96
Be Prepared 97
    Alert servants 98
    Ten virgins 98
    Unclean spirit 99
    Watching slaves 100
    Wise slave 101
    Children in the marketplace 102
    Signs of the end 103
Treasures in Heaven 106
    Hidden treasure 108
    Pearl of great price 109
    Rich man and Lazarus 109
    Rich fool 110
Righteous vs. Sinners 111
    Dinner guests 111
    Feast invitations 112
Jesus' Role 113
    Bread of life 114
    Divided kingdom 115
    Sign of Jonah 117
The Lost 119
    Lost coin 119
    Lost sheep 119
    Prodigal son 120
Sorting Sinners from the Saved 122
    Net of fish 122
    Sheep and goats 123

Landowner	124
Tares in the field	127
Tares in the field (Cont'd.)	128
Disciplines	129
Humbled guest	129
Pharisee and tax collector	130
Servant's duty	130
Unjust steward	131
Talents and pounds	132
Mustard seed	135
Miscellaneous	136
Groom's attendants	136
New cloth	137
New wine	138
King's war plans	138
Salt without taste	139
Afterword	141
Appendix I	143
'Believing in' vs. 'Believing'	143
Appendix II	145
God's Will	145

Introduction

The bad news is: Millions of church members are going to Hell. These are the people who put their faith in 'the church' itself and ignore or forget the teachings of Jesus. They are the people who think that doing church busy work is taking up the cross of Jesus.

The good news is: You can do something about it – on at least two levels.

Christianity in America is involved in the greatest crisis in its history (a battle that is already being lost in many European countries). Tragically, the crisis is at work like a cancer throughout the church, deep and undiagnosed. And many church leaders and members go blithely about their business with no recognition or concern for the battle. Most churches overlook the fact that almost half of all Americans can't name the four gospels. It seems unlikely that those who can't name the gospels have learned much from them. And many, who have read the gospels, steadfastly ignore or forget those teachings of Jesus that are unattractive to them.

John the Baptist came out of the wilderness to prepare the way for Jesus. He preached repentance to Gentiles and other obvious sinners. But his harshest words were for the priests, the wealthy, the leaders of the Jews and others who felt they were righteous. John associated them with murdering the prophets and failing to keep God's commandments. And he called them a brood of vipers.

The brood still exists, inside and outside the church. And the need for repentance is just as great today.

Satan obviously uses a variety of temptations and techniques in his efforts to corrupt and capture the souls of men. He fills men's hearts and minds with greed and lust and self-centeredness, hatred and pride. And most of us can recognize these traits in everyone but ourselves.

In America today, Satan seeks to diminish the fear of Hell by promoting a vision of a government sponsored, or church sponsored, Heaven on earth. He also diminishes the significance of sin. He even encourages some churches to call America a 'Christian nation' despite its crime and greed and immorality.

One of the most effective and insidious weapons in Satan's arsenal is cultivating indifference to Jesus' teachings in men's minds. Atheists and agnostics have little problem in admitting indifference or confusion about the creator god. But they are not Satan's prey, so their indifference is of little interest or benefit to him.

Part of the toll of indifference is taken among the 'casual or occasional Christians' in our churches. Few Americans are as indifferent to their families or their jobs or their sports favorites as many church members are to the teachings of Jesus. Even political and entertainment figures receive more attention from some people in the pews. These indifferent ones include church leaders and members who choose to water down the demands of Jesus to make them more comfortable. Most of us have a hard time recognizing this indifference especially in ourselves.

Another part of the toll is among 'good church members' who 'prove' their faith with church busy work and study and contributions, but only occasionally bother to apply Jesus' teachings.

Both groups worship a church itself and rejoice in the fun of Christmas, and 'hope' they are saved.

One of the roles of prophets in the Judeo-Christian tradition is to scold sinners and hypocrites and call them to repentance and a renewed relationship with the creator god. This book of prophecy is in that same tradition.

This book may be injurious to your peace of mind if you think:

- There really is a creator god
- God really needs your money
- Jesus really was God's son and messenger
- Jesus was serious about the lessons he taught
- There really is a 'heaven' and eternal life
- There really is a Satan
- There really is a 'hell' and eternal damnation
- Church membership guarantees salvation.

Satan is not at all concerned with how much we may read our Bibles, or pray, or praise, or attend church and Sunday school. He doesn't care how much we give to the church, or profess our belief in Jesus. Satan is only concerned when we let those activities change our lives and bring us closer to God in keeping with Jesus' teachings.

As you sit in church, look around you. Are you and the other members really different from people outside 'the church?' Does your relationship with the creator god and with Jesus set you apart from non-Christians in your attitudes and behavior?

"Men are not flattered by being shown that there has been a difference of purpose between the Almighty and them." A. Lincoln

"If the mind discerns new truths incompatible with standing scriptural interpretations, then it is the interpretation that is wrong, not the truth." Augustine

From the time Eve and Adam took their first bites of the forbidden fruit, men and women have been forgetting or ignoring God's rules and teachings. They have killed their brothers, waged wars, created empires, committed adultery and incest, worshipped Mammon and other gods, stolen and lied. And, at the same time, they have sought relationship with the creator god on their own terms instead of on God's terms.

'The church' has played an active part in provoking or condoning much of this behavior. And it has worked for centuries to interpret the scriptures for its own benefit. In the course of this effort, much of what the gospels report about Jesus' life and teachings has been ignored and, in essence, forgotten.

The greatest spiritual challenge for you, and for every individual, is the choice of the god/s you will worship and devote your life to. Judeo-Christian leaders have always approached this challenge by deciding which parts of the scriptures they will take seriously and which they will ignore. You have an opportunity to look again at the gospel teachings and decide which ones you will practice and which gods you will serve.

It's vital for you to determine what's in it for you:

- To accept and believe Jesus and follow his teachings, and
- To accept the costs to you in worldly terms.

As a Christian there are three things you need to know for your eternal wellbeing:

1) The first is that Satan is alive and well and vying for your soul. He works through putting one or more false gods between you and the creator god. These include: gods of possessions (your job, Visa, MasterCard, Wall Street, etc.); gods of amusement (sports, substance abuse, rock concerts, NASCAR, etc.); gods of pride (your own will or ambitions political power, lust, greed, etc.) and others, including many churches.

Satan is still at work in the world. And he doesn't care whether you 'believe in' him or not so long as you keep his commandments:

- You shall put your own interests ahead of God's interests
- You shall put your own interests ahead of other people's interests
- You shall worship wealth and power and self-sufficiency
- You shall worship the appetites and pleasures of the flesh
- You shall challenge and/or ignore the authority of the creator god.

You may find the church's leadership in resisting these tempters is sometimes more detrimental than positive.

Perhaps the most misleading temptation presented by 'the church' is to equate church membership with salvation. To let members believe that church membership, attendance at worship and living 'a good life' assures them of salvation is to rob those members of Christ's promises and assurance. It encourages us to ignore his examples. Often, this practice ignores Jesus' demands. In effect the church risks (and sometimes promotes) having members worship the church and its leaders rather than the creator god. We find ourselves practicing what some wag dubbed 'Churchianity' rather than Christianity. Many Jews in Jesus' time worshipped the gold of the temple instead of the god of the temple.

A second powerful temptation is to emphasize the dogma and traditions of your denomination to the detriment of the gospel. The only justification for the establishment of any denomination (or "non-denominational 'community church'") is to have an understanding of God's actions and intentions that makes that denomination 'right' and every other denomination 'wrong.'

When you choose a denomination you say, in effect, that your group's understanding and obedience to God's will sets it above all other denominations in God's sight and in his service. Some denominations are convinced that anyone who is not a member of their denomination is going to Hell.

As a matter of reality, millions of church members cannot identify those beliefs that set their denomination apart from others. Many of them don't care. They are more conscious of differences in practices (such as the use of wine for communion, or kneeling, or total immersion for baptism).

If you can believe that Methodists, Baptists, Catholics, Presbyterians and other 'Christian groups' are equally close to the creator god, you are denying the validity of your denomination and others. The whole history of denominational conflicts is surely an embarrassment for God and a hindrance for his plans. And, for some, the worship of their denomination approaches idolatry.

2) The second thing you need to know is that the creator god still offers salvation to those who will receive it and demonstrate their faith by obeying the teachings of Jesus.

I'm embarrassed for God that men are still 'discovering' his will 2,000 years after Jesus' resurrection. And I'm embarrassed that so many church members act as if grace is not only free but that it's cheap as well.

Jesus taught both by word and by example, demonstrating his surrender to and dependence on the creator god. When Jesus was killed it was not because of his teachings alone. It was because he demonstrated his relationship with the creator god, and this was even more of a threat to the religious leaders of his time than were his teachings. But if awareness of Jesus' teachings and the practice of those teachings were made conditions of church membership today there would be no church as we know it.

The primary purpose of Jesus' teachings and of Christian study is not to increase our knowledge, but to change our behavior. It is to show men the way to build relationships

with the creator god and their fellow men. If your worship and study do not change your life they may very well be a waste of your time and Jesus' sacrifice for your soul.

3) The third thing you need to know is that Jesus will not force you to follow him.

Your personal challenge is to decide what following Jesus involves, what it requires of you, and whether you think it is worth paying the price. Remember, saying you 'believe in' Jesus Christ doesn't count for a thing if you ignore or neglect his teachings and examples.

This book you're reading does not look to 'recently discovered' works such as 'The Gospel of Thomas' or 'The Gospel of Judas' to find neglected and forgotten teachings. Instead it looks to the four gospels that 50 or more generations of 'Christians' have proclaimed to be the word of their god. The gospels give men more information than we need in our pursuit of the creator god. Jesus used parables to confound the casual and indifferent among his listeners. Thousands of those who heard Jesus teach were perfectly nice people, good friends to their friends, active in their synagogues, faithful to the rules of the temple and deaf to his demands. Too many members of 'the church' today are still essentially casual and indifferent to Jesus' demands and promises. Instead, they choose the comfort and convenience of a 'religious community' rather than the challenge of the cross. Unfortunately, if a congregation of people does not obey Jesus' teachings they are not truly a part of his church.

The gospels also tell us that the creator god does not love everyone who 'believes in' Jesus but that he loves those who 'believe' Jesus. (For a discussion of the difference between 'believing in' Jesus and 'believing' Jesus, see Appendix I.) And, of course, while God offers his love to everyone his love is essentially meaningless for those who don't care or respond.

For almost 2000 years the church's practice has often been contradictory to Jesus' commands and examples. Too often our behavior makes Jesus' life and death look like a waste of God's time and effort.

Jesus' true appeal is still to sinners and not to the self-righteous. The latter, of course, may dominate many congregations today just as they dominated the temple and many synagogues in Jesus' day. In truth, many church members don't take Jesus' teachings seriously even if they know of them. We tend to treat Jesus' teachings like fairy tales: entertaining and idealistic, but not to be taken so seriously that we're embarrassed or inconvenienced by their practice. Oftentimes individuals and families join a congregation for financial or political reasons or for the fellowship it provides, rather than the challenge it presents.

Preachers/ministers/priests and other religious bureaucrats sometimes come to love and encourage the people's dependence on them and their teachings. They encourage dependence on the dogma and ritual and buildings and programs and traditions of 'the church.' They too often endorse and/or encourage members' willingness to accept this *faux* faith as bona fide relationship with Jesus Christ.

Despite generations of Christian education, the church has a problem. In his challenging book *Jesus* Marcus J. Borg cites a poll reporting that "over 80 percent of Americans identify themselves as Christian, well over 200 million people." Borg says the same poll reports that "only 48 percent (of Americans) could name the gospels."

If God has created a hunger for growth and relationship in your heart, read on. But, if you're perfectly content with your relationship with your god/s and content with your Christian growth, you're not likely to find much comfort or wisdom in this book.

Only you can change how you respond to Jesus and to the creator god.

You owe it to yourself to deal with these questions:

- What are the benefits of applying Jesus' teachings?
- What is the cost of applying these teachings?
- What is the cost of ignoring these teachings?

- What will I do about these teachings?

Some of Jesus' forgotten teachings are presented here in parallel as they appear in one or more of the gospels.

Faith

The gospels make it clear that Jesus' ministry was not about accumulating wealth or power or prestige. In fact, he was committed to opposing the abuses inflicted on the poor by those who pursued these goals. Instead, his whole focus was on building an individual's faith in, and relationship with, the creator god and other men.

If you get nothing else from this book, please understand that faith is not just what you believe. Faith is what you do. No matter how much you study or pray or sing or give to the church, you cannot experience the creator god unless you live according to his will.

The gospels mention the word church one time in a meaningful way.[1] The gospels tell us nothing about how this 'church' was to behave or how it was to be structured. They say nothing about impressive buildings. But they do tell us what the church's objectives were and how the church was to be financed. The early Christians understood themselves as constituting a church. No doubt they perceived themselves as called out by God in Jesus Christ for a special purpose. And they believed their status was a privileged one in Jesus Christ.

But the gospels stress the concept of faith dozens of times. And the concept is clearly what Jesus was concerned with. It was, and is, the key to miracles in this life and to eternal life. Faith is also your key to serving the creator god and avoiding the Hell of separation from him.

---

[1] Matt. 16:18

It may help to recognize that faith operates in at least two dimensions. In one dimension, faith prepares us to do the work Jesus calls us to.

Matt. 17: 20 He said to them, "Because of your little faith. For truly I tell you, if you have faith the size of a mustard seed, you will say to this mountain, 'Move from here to there,' and it will move; and nothing will be impossible for you."	Mark 11: 22 Jesus answered them, "Have faith in God.	Luke 17: 6 The Lord replied, "If you had faith the size of a mustard seed, you could say to this mulberry tree, 'Be uprooted and planted in the sea,' and it would obey you."	
Matt. 21: 21 Jesus answered them, "Truly I tell you, if you have faith and do not doubt, not only will you do what has been done to the fig tree,	23 Truly I tell you, if you say to this mountain, 'Be taken up and thrown into the sea,' and if you do not doubt in your heart, but believe that		

but even if you say to this mountain, 'Be lifted up and thrown into the sea,' it will be done. 22 Whatever you ask for in prayer with faith, you will receive."	what you say will come to pass, it will be done for you. 24 So I tell you, whatever you ask for in prayer, believe that you have received it, and it will be yours." Mark 16: 17 "And these signs will accompany those who believe: by using my name they will cast out demons; they will speak in new tongues; 18 they will pick up snakes in their hands, and if they drink any deadly thing, it will not hurt them; they will lay their		John 14: 12 "Very truly, I tell you, the one who believes in me will also do the works that I do and, in fact, will do greater works than these, because I am going to the Father."

| | hands on the sick, and they will recover." | | |

Jesus commissioned more than 70 of the faithful to go out ahead of him and work miracles of healing, even raising the dead. He also promised that future followers could work similar miracles. Jesus knew the value of his miracles as a testimony to his relationship with the creator god. And he knew his followers would need the same sort of testimony if their teachings about faith and relationship were to be taken seriously.

It's worth noting that these followers, and the disciples, did not insist on pastoral contracts or guarantees of any kind other than Jesus' promises. And many of them left family and possessions behind when they went out to spread the good news.

In a second dimension, faith prepares us to receive the blessings God has prepared for us.

Time after time Jesus demonstrated that the creator god was willing and able to meet the needs of the faithful on a day-to-day basis. God fed Jesus and the disciples for three years just as he fed thousands of Jews in the wilderness for 40 years. God fed thousands of Jesus' listeners with only a few loaves and fishes. And there's no report of Jesus taking up a collection to meet his expenses. It's fair to suggest that many of our prayers today remain unanswered because of our lack of faith and our lack of surrender to God's will.

There is no record of Jesus healing the afflictions that doctors of his day could deal with. But the gospels are full of instances when Jesus rewarded the faith of followers and even strangers (Jew and Gentile) with miraculous healing of 'incurable' afflictions.

Nowhere do the gospels tell us that Jesus refused to help petitioners because it was God's will. Nor does he tell the faithful to wait for relief.

The people of Israel didn't come out to hear Jesus teach just because he made such good sense. His ideas were as radical then as they are today. Mostly the people came out of curiosity. And they came because of the miraculous things he and his followers were doing: healing the sick, giving sight to the blind, casting out demons, raising the dead and feeding thousands. And hundreds, perhaps thousands of people, came to be healed.

The letters of the apostles and contemporary history suggest that believers continued to work miracles for several years, perhaps a couple of centuries. But, when Constantine vested the Church of Rome with legitimacy and POWER, the evidence of miracles declined. Now church leaders could <u>command</u> the attention Jesus and the disciples had attracted with mighty works. And those leaders could present church membership, in the guise of faith, as the path to survival and salvation.

And when Constantine built the original (old) St. Peter's Basilica, he gave the church a god to worship, a god they could see and touch, just as the Jews worshiped the golden calf in the wilderness. He prompted an emphasis on big and impressive buildings which has absorbed congregations for generations.

Over time the church took the authority to define the scriptures. And church leaders carefully selected or edited teachings to agree with their own beliefs. Perhaps only the human hunger for miracles among church members caused the church fathers to retain passages such as we have here, though the verses were certainly useful in attracting people to 'the church.' Through the centuries, many church leaders have reduced the passages to the status of wishful thinking or myth. Indeed, some modern collections of 'Bible promises' don't even mention many of the passages that promise miracles.

John 17: 1 After Jesus had spoken these words, he looked up to heaven and said, "Father, the hour has come; glorify your Son so that the Son may glorify you,

2 since you have given him authority over all people, to give

> eternal life to all whom you have given him.
>
> 3 And this is eternal life, that they may know you, the only true God, and Jesus Christ whom you have sent.
>
> 4 I glorified you on earth by finishing the work that you gave me to do.
>
> 5 So now, Father, glorify me in your own presence with the glory that I had in your presence before the world existed.
>
> 6 "I have made your name known to those whom you gave me from the world. They were yours, and you gave them to me, and they have kept your word.
>
> 7 Now they know that everything you have given me is from you;
>
> 8 for the words that you gave to me I have given to them, and they have received them and know in truth that I came from you; and they have believed that you sent me.
>
> 9 I am asking on their behalf; I am not asking on behalf of the world, but on behalf of those whom you gave me, because they are yours.
>
> 10 All mine are yours, and yours are mine; and I have been glorified in them.
>
> 11 And now I am no longer in the world, but they are in the world, and I am coming to you. Holy Father, protect them in your name that you have given me, so that they may be one, as we are one.

The disciple John was supposedly one of those who accompanied Jesus when he went to pray in the garden on the night he was captured by the soldiers and temple guards. Yet, John's gospel makes no mention of Jesus' prayer for escape from the cross.

Indeed, John makes Jesus sound almost joyful at his departure from the world.

John also gives us a seldom-quoted definition of eternal life. And he narrows the field of god's love from 'the world' to a much smaller body of those who keep God's word.

| Matt. 26: 36 Then Jesus went with them to a place called Gethsemane; and he said to his disciples, "Sit here while I go over there and pray." 37 He took with him Peter and the two sons of Zebedee, and began to be grieved and agitated. 38 Then he said to them, "I am deeply grieved, even to death; remain here, and stay awake with me." 39 And going a little farther, he threw himself on the ground and prayed, "My Father, if it is possible, let this cup pass from me; yet not what I want but what you want." | Mark 14: 32 They went to a place called Gethsemane; and he said to his disciples, "Sit here while I pray." 33 He took with him Peter and James and John, and began to be distressed and agitated. 34 And said to them, "I am deeply grieved, even to death; remain here, and keep awake." 35 And going a little farther, he threw himself on the ground and prayed that, if it were possible, the hour might pass from him. 36 He said, "Abba, Father, for you all things are possible; remove this cup from me; yet, not | Luke 22: 40 When he reached the place, he said to them, "Pray that you may not come into the time of trial." 41 Then he withdrew from them about a stone's throw, knelt down, and prayed, 42 "Father, if you are willing, remove this cup from me; yet, not my will but yours be done." 43 Then an angel from heaven appeared to him |

	what I want, but what you want."	and gave him strength.
40 Then he came to the disciples and found them sleeping; and he said to Peter, "So, could you not stay awake with me one hour? 41 Stay awake and pray that you may not come into the time of trial; the spirit indeed is willing, but the flesh is weak." 42 Again he went away for the second time and prayed, "My Father, if this cannot pass unless I drink it, your will be done." 43 Again he came and found them sleeping, for their eyes were heavy. 44 So leaving them again, he went away and prayed for the third time, saying the same words. 45 Then he came to the disciples and said to them, "Are you still sleeping	37 He came and found them sleeping; and he said to Peter, "Simon, are you asleep? Could you not keep awake one hour? 38 Keep awake and pray that you may not come into the time of trial; the spirit indeed is willing, but the flesh is weak." 39 And again he went away and prayed, saying the same words. 40 And once more he came and found them sleeping, for their eyes were very heavy; and they did not know what to say to him. 41 He came a third time and said to them, "Are you still sleeping and taking	Luke 22: 45 When he got up from prayer, he came to the disciples and found them sleeping because of grief, 46 and he said to them, "Why are you sleeping? Get up and pray that you may not come into the time of trial."

and taking your rest? See, the hour is at hand, and the Son of Man is betrayed into the hands of sinners."	your rest? Enough! The hour has come; the Son of Man is betrayed into the hands of sinners. 42 Get up, let us be going. See, my betrayer is at hand."

For centuries the leaders of 'the church' have used these passages to explain failed prayers as being the result of 'God's will.' They excuse the lack of faith on their own part and on the part of their congregations by blaming God. It's appropriate to ask whether your faith gets your prayers answered.

We'll never know if the church fathers invented these passages to justify their own failures. But we can be sure the verses are hard to explain and completely inconsistent with the body of Jesus' teachings. And they paint Jesus as a far weaker person than he proved to be.

The question arises, "Why would men worship a Jesus with no miracles?" The answer, too often, is that they don't worship him at all but worship the church instead.

Your challenge is to decide what your god demands of you and whether the price is worth paying.

The Greatest Commandments

No aspect of Jesus' ministry was more important to him and to us than the establishment or reestablishment of our relationship with the creator god and with our fellow men. For centuries the Jews and other peoples had worshipped wealth and power and independence in a variety of guises. In effect they were worshipping Mammon through the gods they invented to satisfy their own desires for godship. And the wealthy and other leaders, including the priests and lawyers and rabbies, were exploiting the poor. Jesus, like John the Baptist, came to call men to repentance and reformation. Jesus, of course, also promised that men would experience this life in a more rewarding way. And he promised they would experience eternal life if they kept God's commandments

Despite 2000 years of exposure to Jesus' teachings, men (inside and outside the church) still build their own idols and temples, and they continue to ignore God's commandments and exploit or ignore the poor.

	Mark 12: 28 One of the scribes came near and heard them disputing with one another, and seeing that he answered them well, he asked him,	
Matt. 22: 36 "Teacher, which	"Which commandment is	

commandment in the law is the greatest?" 37 He said to him, "'You shall love the Lord your God with all your heart, and with all your soul, and with all your mind.' 38 This is the greatest and first commandment. 39 And a second is like it: 'You shall love your neighbor as yourself.' On these two commandments hang all the law and the prophets."	the first of all?" 29 Jesus answered, "The first is, 'Hear, O Israel: the Lord our God, the Lord is one; 30 you shall love the Lord your God with all your heart, and with all your soul, and with all your mind, and with all your strength.' 31 The second is this, 'You shall love your neighbor as yourself'. There is no other commandment greater than these."	John 13: 34 "I give you a new commandment, that you love one another. Just as I have loved you, you also should love one another. 35 By this everyone will know that you are my disciples, if you have love for one another." John 15: 12 "This is my commandment, that you love one another as I have loved you." John 15: 17 "I am giving you these

		commands so that you may love one another."

Jesus distilled the Ten Commandments into two.

To love the Lord your God with all your heart and soul and mind and strength is totally unrealistic. It flies in the face of original sin and personal pride. This love goes far beyond being 'a good church member.' It means total surrender to God's will. It means trusting god to keep his promises even without our help. The total focus of the teaching is on love—in capital letters.

But, instead of this all-forgiving and all-encompassing love, the church has sponsored holy wars, crusades, inquisitions, witch hunts and a multitude of other villainies. A bit of graffito from the Korean War summarizes the 'Christian church' attitude over 17 centuries: "Kill a Commie for Christ." Just as the Jews redesigned God every time they needed an excuse for their actions, church leaders have reshaped the creator god to support and excuse democracy, capitalism, white supremacy and a multitude of other causes. Over the years the cry has been: "Kill a Catholic," or "Kill a Protestant," or "Kill a Jew," or redskin or Mormon or pagan.

Too often 'the church' has given Christianity a bad name.

Actually, the commandment to love our neighbors was not new.[2] But it had been ignored for so long that it seemed new and radical to Jesus' audiences just as it seems new and radical to church members today.

What we seldom appreciate is the fact that our ability to respect and love others is a reflection of our ability to respect and love ourselves. And love for our neighbors is a floodgate that controls the flow of God's love into our own lives. Only as we let love flow out of us to our neighbors can God's love flow in.

---

[2] Leviticus 19: 18.

You have an opportunity to reconsider what loving your neighbor means to you. Can you love your enemies as much as you love your friends? As much as you love yourself?

Make a list of the people you most dislike. Practice asking God to love you as much as you love them.

(See also the parable of the Good Samaritan: p. 84.)

You Must Be Born Again

Jesus' teachings make it abundantly clear that being his follower is not 'doing business as usual.' It goes beyond doing what everyone else is doing, with a church service thrown in occasionally. It is obvious that Jesus expected something significant (a birth of the spirit) to happen to a man or woman when they devoted their lives to spreading his message. Presumably this 'something significant' sets his followers apart from those who have not experienced it. Certainly it goes before and beyond mere baptism, even by immersion.

There is little in the gospels to describe what this 'something significant' amounts to. Neither the disciples, nor other followers recounted the ecstatic, sometimes hysterical, 'infilling' or 'possession' so popular in many revival settings. Paul's blinding experience on the road to Damascus is one of the few reports that comes close.

The experience in the upper room on the Day of Pentecost is obviously special.[3] The men and women gathered there, including some disciples, were already devoted followers of Jesus who were, presumably, already 'born again.' But the manifestation of the Holy Spirit was obviously something much more dramatic than any spiritual rebirth they may have already experienced. Indeed, many Pentecostal denominations today consider this 'baptism with the Holy Spirit' a whole new and superior level of relationship with God. Unfortunately, the modern experience doesn't always result in a superior level of behavior or fruitfulness.

---

[3] Acts 2: 1-41.

Perhaps the common denominator for meaningful conversions is the powerful and persistent assurance of relationship with the creator god that accompanies the 'born again' experience for many converts. For many, the experience is also accompanied by a very real change of attitude (repentance) and behavior (reformation).

What does 'knowing God and Jesus' mean to you in terms of how you live?

If you have been a church member for forty years, or twenty years, or ten or even two years and don't feel some such change and assurance, how has your salvation impacted your life? If you feel no such assurance, there's good reason to wonder whether you are 'born again.' **And, finding that assurance is key to your Christian growth and service.**

John 3: 16 "For God so loved the world that he gave his only Son, so that everyone who believes in him may not perish but may have eternal life."

John 14: 6 Jesus said to him, "I am the way, and the truth, and the life. No one comes to the Father except through me."

John 17: 3 "And this is eternal life, that they may know you, the only true God, and Jesus Christ whom you have sent."

John 20: 31 But these are written so that you may come to believe that Jesus is the Messiah, the Son of God, and that through believing you may have life in his name.

The prospect of eternal life in communion with the creator god is, perhaps, the primary justification for anyone's becoming a Christian. Indeed, renewing that communion is God's reason for sending Jesus to Earth and to his death. Part of the bad news is that such a prospect is less compelling for many people who are self-sufficient. Part of the good news, often overlooked, is that eternal life and Heaven begin when you are reborn, not after you die.

Unfortunately, too many 'born again' believers look only to the 'heavenly' time after their body dies. They ignore the challenge to grow in their new life. And, they miss many opportunities for service to the creator god in their new relationships.

Some reasonable self-tests of whether you or any church member are/is reborn or not might include: "Are you afraid to die?" or "Are you absolutely sure that your sins have been forgiven?" or "Are you sure that you have been saved?" or "How has being reborn made your life noticeably different from the lives of those who haven't been born again?" If you're afraid to die or if you're unsure of your salvation how can you enjoy the blessings of salvation? How can you share Jesus with someone else? How are you more blessed than someone outside the church?

Surely it was some such assurance that empowered the revered martyrs in the Roman church to go to the lions with a hymn on their lips.

Goodness and niceness and humanitarianism and a sense of community are wonderful things. They obviously serve to support and justify some churches and/or other service/charitable/social organizations. These qualities were also the life-blood of Jewish society and many pagan cultures in Jesus' day and throughout history. But, without repentance, salvation/rebirth and reformation, any promises those organizations may make of life with the creator god are empty.

John 3: 3 Jesus answered him, "Very truly, I tell you, no one can see the kingdom of God without being born from above."

4 Nicodemus said to him, "How can anyone be born after having grown old? Can one enter a second time into the mother's womb and be born?"

5 Jesus answered, "Very truly, I tell you, no one can enter the

> kingdom of God without being born of water and Spirit.
>
> 6 What is born of the flesh is flesh, and what is born of the Spirit is spirit.
>
> 7 Do not be astonished that I said to you, 'You must be born from above.'
>
> 8 The wind blows where it chooses, and you hear the sound of it, but you do not know where it comes from or where it goes. So it is with everyone who is born of the Spirit."
>
> 9 Nicodemus said to him, "How can these things be?"
>
> 10 Jesus answered him, "Are you a teacher of Israel, and yet you do not understand these things?
>
> 11 Very truly, I tell you, we speak of what we know and testify to what we have seen; yet you do not receive our testimony.
>
> 12 If I have told you about earthly things and you do not believe, how can you believe if I tell you about heavenly things?
>
> 13 No one has ascended into heaven except the one who descended from heaven, the Son of Man.
>
> 14 And just as Moses lifted up the serpent in the wilderness, so must the Son of Man be lifted up,
>
> 15 that whoever believes in him may have eternal life."

Most Americans know where and when they were born and who their parents were. They have memories of graduations and marriages and other milestones, especially life-changing events. In many cases these events were followed by periods of growth and/or change. Jesus told Nicodemus that he needed to experience an equally dramatic new birth of the spirit.

New birth is a totally new concept in the New Testament with no apparent roots in the Old Testament, but Jesus seemed surprised that Nicodemus, a Pharisee and a leader of the Jews, could not grasp the life-changing nature of this concept.

Today, many church members have little more than a fuzzy understanding of rebirth, and many denominations seem to treat it as laughable or unsophisticated, sometimes even threatening. Many individuals who truly feel they have experienced rebirth seem to regard it as the end of a process rather than the beginning. They neglect the growth that should follow the new birth. Unfortunately, too, many 'born again Christians' are not even excited enough about their salvation to share their experience with others.

> John 5: 24 "Very truly, I tell you, anyone who hears my word and believes him who sent me has eternal life, and does not come under judgment, but has passed from death to life."
>
> John 6: 47 "Very truly, I tell you, whoever believes has eternal life."
>
> John 11: 25 Jesus said to her, "I am the resurrection and the life. Those who believe in me, even though they die, will live,
> 26 and everyone who lives and believes in me will never die. Do you believe this?"

I have a friend who had a heart attack several years ago. As he was being released from the hospital, a nurse said, "We've given you a life, it's up to you to decide what you will do with it." In a very real way, God gives us a new life when we are born again and it is up to us to determine what we will do with it.

You owe it to yourself to know what this 'new birth' means to you, how it impacts your life, what you expect of it and what kind of price tag this new life carries.

Your body and mind need nourishment and exercise for healthy growth. When you are 'born again' your new life also needs a regimen of nourishment and exercise for healthy growth.

You need to decide whether your experience with God and Jesus and the Holy Spirit really makes a difference in your life and makes your life different from what it was like before your rebirth, and how it is different from the lives of people who claim no such experience.

Write down your thoughts about your 'new birth' and what it means to you.

How have you grown since your rebirth?

Witness

During his ministry, Jesus performed many miraculous works. He healed the sick, raised the dead, fed thousands with almost nothing, put gold in the mouth of a fish, calmed storms and walked on water. But, wonderful as they were, these 'miracles' were not the core of his mission. Jesus did these 'works' to demonstrate his authority to the disciples and others who saw and heard him. He promised that those who believed him would be able to do similar or greater works, and many of his followers did miracles during his lifetime. But those miracles (and other so-called 'spiritual gifts') were not the core of their mission either.

> Luke 10: 1 After this the Lord appointed seventy others and sent them on ahead of him in pairs to every town and place where he himself intended to go.
> 2 He said to them, "The harvest is plentiful, but the laborers are few; therefore ask the Lord of the harvest to send out laborers into his harvest.
> 3 Go on your way. See, I am sending you out like lambs into the midst of wolves.
> 4 Carry no purse, no bag, no sandals; and greet no one on the road.
> 5 Whatever house you enter, first say, 'Peace to this house!'
> 6 And if anyone is there who shares in peace, your peace will rest on that person; but if not, it will return to you.
> 7 Remain in the same house, eating and drinking whatever they provide, for the laborer deserves to be paid. Do not move about from house to house.
> 8 Whenever you enter a town and its people welcome you, eat what is set before you;
> 9 cure the sick who are there, and say to them, 'The kingdom of

> God has come near to you.'
> 10 But whenever you enter a town and they do not welcome you, go out into its streets and say,
> 11 'Even the dust of your town that clings to our feet, we wipe off in protest against you. Yet know this: the kingdom of God has come near.'
> 12 I tell you, on that day it will be more tolerable for Sodom than for that town.
> 13 "Woe to you, Chorazin! Woe to you, Bethsaida! For if the deeds of power done in you had been done in Tyre and Sidon, they would have repented long ago, sitting in sackcloth and ashes.
> 14 But at the judgment it will be more tolerable for Tyre and Sidon than for you.
> 15 And you, Capernaum, will you be exalted to heaven? No, you will be brought down to Hades.
> 16 Whoever listens to you listens to me, and whoever rejects you rejects me, and whoever rejects me rejects the one who sent me."
> 17 The seventy returned with joy, saying, "Lord, in your name even the demons submit to us!"
> 18 He said to them, "I watched Satan fall from heaven like a flash of lightning."

It's almost frightening to modern church members that seventy people who followed Jesus at a distance could believe him strongly enough to fulfill this commission. He sent them out without contracts, without red carpets, without organ music or even guitars. They took only the bare essentials and were empowered to perform miracles of healing and to preach the good news. Equally frightening is the promise of damnation for those who rejected the messengers.

Jesus did not call his followers to feed, or heal, or entertain or comfort multitudes of pagans or even church members. He didn't call them to build beautiful and/or pretentious, congregation-glorifying buildings of glass and stone. He didn't call them to slaughter anyone who questioned their beliefs, or to build kingdoms on earth, though these things have surely been done in his name.

> Matt. 28: 19 "Go therefore and make disciples of all nations, baptizing them in the name of the Father and of the Son and of the Holy Spirit,
> 20 and teaching them to obey everything that I have commanded you. And remember, I am with you always, to the end of the age."
>
> John 15: 27 "You also are to testify because you have been with me from the beginning."
>
> John 21: 15 When they had finished breakfast, Jesus said to Simon Peter, "Simon son of John, do you love me more than these?" He said to him, "Yes, Lord; you know that I love you." Jesus said to him, "Feed my lambs."
> 16 A second time he said to him, "Simon son of John, do you love me?" He said to him, "Yes, Lord; you know that I love you." Jesus said to him, "Tend my sheep."
> 17 He said to him the third time, "Simon son of John, do you love me?" Peter felt hurt because he said to him the third time, "Do you love me?" And he said to him, "Lord, you know everything; you know that I love you." Jesus said to him, "Feed my sheep.
>
> Acts 1: 8 "But you will receive power when the Holy Spirit has come upon you; and you will be my witnesses in Jerusalem, in all Judea and Samaria, and to the ends of the earth."
>
> Acts 14: 3 So they remained for a long time, speaking boldly for the Lord, who testified to the word of his grace by granting signs and wonders to be done through them.

Jesus' mission was to call sinners, and other people with problems, to repentance and to a renewed and passionate, if radical, relationship with the creator god: to heal men's souls. Despite the apparent belief of some modern churches, Jesus did not say that everyone would be saved. In fact, he denies this idea several times. Matt. 28: 19 tells followers to make disciples in every nation, not to make everyone a disciple.

And he charged his followers with continuing this mission and extending it throughout the world. The process obviously goes beyond merely ministering to the physical needs of the sick and the hungry of the world (though modern churches don't always do a very good job of that either). He wants us to feed sinners the bread of life.

History suggests that the repentance and radical relationship Jesus encouraged may have pervaded the underground church for about 300 years. The church thrived on evangelism and persecution. But, with the endorsement of Constantine, the focus of the church began to change dramatically. And, given man's lust for wealth and power, the focus has seldom, if ever, been the same. No longer persecuted and forced into hiding, 'the church' quickly began to put the idea of suffering for the faith behind it.

Unfortunately, and understandably, the spiritual gifts also seem to have declined at about the same time. Instead of relying on miracles to attract sinners and support converts, the church learned to rely on political power, fear, and impressive displays of wealth and ritual and entertainment to attract and control members. Instead of praying for its enemies the church learned to slaughter them. Only groups that disagreed with the Roman Church fathers would experience such persecution.

And salvation often became synonymous with church membership, with little or no concern for repentance or reformation.

For centuries the church has interpreted the promise of miraculous answers to prayer as subject to the whim of God. In many passages, Jesus stresses for his followers that miracles are dependent on their faith and not just on God's will.

Obviously, the commission for witness was not just to the eleven disciples. The charge was to all believers in all ages. Unfortunately, many 'believers' have abdicated their responsibility and left witnessing to religious professionals. In modern America, church members are often suspicious of or even frightened by people (such as the Mormons or Jehovah's Witnesses) who witness openly. Sometimes this is because we are so poorly prepared to present or defend our own faith. Sometimes it's because we have so little to share.

Millions of church members; who can talk for hours about their children, their work, sports, entertainment, politics or their church; have little or nothing to say about their relationship with Jesus Christ. And many of us are uncomfortable around others, including fellow church members or ministers, who do.

Too many churches measure their success by the number of members they have recruited rather than by the number of sinners they have lead to salvation. If your church is not preparing you and inspiring you to witness to Jesus Christ then it is failing in its mission to the creator god and to you.

It's appropriate to ask yourself: "How much does Jesus mean to me if I can't (or won't) even share him with others? Do I have anything to share?" If a friend asked you to tell him/her about your relationship with Jesus, what would you say?

A helpful exercise is to write down just how you came to accept the salvation Jesus offers and how that acceptance has changed your life.

The second level on which you can glorify the creator god and oppose Satan is by doing the one thing that only Christians can do, that is by sharing Jesus with others. It is also the most wonderful and/or threatening gift you can give another person.

Are you doing what God expects of you?

List the people you would share salvation with if you could.

Temptations from Satan

The following passages tell us a great deal about two of the principal players in the gospels. They also speak to individuals and to 'the church' today.

Did Jesus reveal this episode to the disciples? Or did the gospel writers invent the temptations that would be most likely to confront followers?

The passages reveal the kinds of temptations that still confront us:

- Living our lives in pursuit of pleasures of the flesh
- Testing or challenging God to keep his word
- And living our lives in pursuit of wealth and power.

I've included the passages to remind us that Jesus teaches us by his example as well as by his words. They serve to remind us of the powerful temptations we face every day. They also remind us that Satan is still active in our world.

Matt. 4: 3 The tempter came and said to him, "If you are the Son of God, command these stones to become loaves of bread."	Luke 4: 3 The devil said to him, "If you are the Son of God, command this stone to become a loaf of bread."
4 But he answered, "It is written, 'One does not live by bread alone, but by every word that comes from the mouth of God.'"	4 Jesus answered him, "It is written, 'One does not live by bread alone.'"

Jesus obviously put the teachings of God above creature comforts, even including food. He makes clear that God's word is more sustaining for men than bread. This reality surely justifies our determination to live in accord with Jesus' teachings.

It's worth noting that Satan could quote Old Testament scripture with the best of fundamentalist preachers. Jesus, of course, put a new interpretation on the words.

Matt. 4: 5 Then the devil took him to the holy city and placed him on the pinnacle of the temple, 6 saying to him, "If you are the Son of God, throw yourself down; for it is written, 'He will command his angels concerning you,' and 'On their hands they will bear you up, so that you will not dash your foot against a stone.'" 7 Jesus said to him, "Again it is written, 'Do not put the Lord your God to the test.'"	Luke 4: 9 Then the devil took him to Jerusalem, and placed him on the pinnacle of the temple, saying to him, "If you are the Son of God, throw yourself down from here, 10 for it is written, 'He will command his angels concerning you, to protect you,' 11 and 'On their hands they will bear you up, so that you will not dash your foot against a stone.'" 12 Jesus answered him, "It is said, 'Do not put the Lord your God to the test.'"

This is surely a hard lesson to accept since so many of our prayers seem to put God on the spot. Indeed, many of Jesus' promises seem to encourage just that. The passage, however, probably cautions against questioning the reality and power of the creator god. The critical factor, in any case, is not God's faithfulness but the faithfulness of the person praying.

Matt. 4: 8 Again, the devil took him to a very high mountain and showed him all the	Luke 4: 5 Then the devil led him up and showed him in an instant all the kingdoms of the

kingdoms of the world and their splendor; 9 and he said to him, "All these I will give you, if you will fall down and worship me."	world. 6 And the devil said to him, "To you I will give their glory and all this authority; for it has been given over to me, and I give it to anyone I please. 7 If you, then, will worship me, it will all be yours."
10 Jesus said to him, "Away with you, Satan! for it is written, 'Worship the Lord your God, and serve only him.'"	8 Jesus answered him, "It is written, 'Worship the Lord your God, and serve only him.'"

The passages tell us a great deal about Satan and about God. According to this section, it is Satan who has control over the wealth and power of this world (though we're not told how he received this authority). And this is consistent with what we often see in our world and even in some of today's churches. The passages also call in question which god 'the church' and its members have been worshipping for the past 1800 years. Nothing we see today suggests that Christianity, as we know it, has changed the world.

You owe it to yourself to know when you have been exposed to these temptations, how you have responded to them, the price you have paid or will pay, and when and how you will make any corrections that you might need to make.

List the things most likely to tempt you.

Take up Your Cross

Many church members today seem to regard taking up Jesus' cross as a 'stroll in the park.' They follow a Jesus who promises abundance and happiness and air-conditioned comfort and high-tech church entertainment to anyone who might say he 'believes in' Jesus. There is little in the radical teachings of Jesus to support such expectations, but there are many churches and other religious organizations which strive to encourage such beliefs.

| Matt. 10: 38 "and whoever does not take up the cross and follow me is not worthy of me. 39 Those who find their life will lose it, and those who lose their life for my sake will find it."

 Matt. 16: 24 Then Jesus told his disciples, "If any want to become my followers, let them deny themselves and take up their cross and follow me." | Mark 8: 34 He called the crowd with his disciples, and said to them, "If any want to become my followers, let them deny themselves and take up their cross and follow me." | Luke 9: 23 Then he said to them all, "If any want to become my followers, let them deny themselves and take up their cross daily and follow me. 24 For those who want to save their life will lose it, and those who lose their life for my sake will save it."

 Luke 14: 27 "Whoever does not carry the cross and follow me cannot be my disciple." |

Since the days of Constantine 'the church' has been tempted to make popularity a primary goal. Today the temptation is so strong that many church leaders feel it necessary to entertain their congregations and to make Christian worship 'fun,' with many of the aspects of a rock concert.

The gospels use the expression 'deny themselves' repeatedly. The disciples understood this to involve sacrifice and, perhaps, suffering and death. They left their families and their jobs and even their countries to share Jesus with others. Most of them died for their commitment. Many of the saints we sometimes revere also suffered for their witness. These careers were a far cry from the contractual security and comfort so many church leaders enjoy today. They were even farther from the teachings of the so-called 'Prosperity Gospel' so popular today.

Taking up your cross is more than putting a cross on a gold chain or on a string around your neck and wearing it like an ornament or a talisman. It is more than having a catchy bumper sticker on your car. Jesus cautioned that such behavior has its reward on earth. And he also suggested that such behavior has nothing to do with the heavenly rewards he promised.

Your challenge is to decide whether Jesus was serious about taking up the cross; what taking up the cross means for you; whether the rewards are worth it to you; and what adjusting your behavior, if necessary, would mean for your life.

Write out what "taking up Jesus' cross" has meant for you or what it would mean for you.

The Sermon on the Mount and Parallels

It's important to remember that Jesus' mission was to the vast multitudes of Jews who had been impoverished and dominated by the wealthy and other Jewish leaders, including their priests. And the foundation of the leaders' wealth depended on maintaining good relations with their Roman masters.

Obviously, an itinerant preacher like Jesus used the same material with many audiences in many settings. The gospel writers surely collected the teachings they thought summarized Jesus' message and reported them in collections such as this sermon. Luke reports many of the teachings that parallel those found in Matthew.

Beatitudes

The word read as blessed is often translated as happy or blissful.

Matt. 5: 3 "Blessed are the poor in spirit, for theirs is the kingdom of heaven."	Luke 6: 20 Then he looked up at his disciples and said: "Blessed are you who are poor, for yours is the kingdom of God."

Jesus begins his sermon with a promise of heaven to those humble enough to surrender to God and depend on him rather than on their own wealth and accomplishments. For many poor Jews this may have been the only viable option.

Like the following promises this presumes that those who hear Jesus believe him and accept his promise of rebirth.

The almost-common element in the beatitudes is the demand for surrender of our own self-interests to God's will.

| Matt. 5: 4 "Blessed are those who mourn, for they will be comforted." | Luke 6: 21 "Blessed are you who weep now, for you will laugh." |

He follows with a promise to those who mourn for their own sins and for the lost sinners among the Jews.

| Matt. 5: 5 "Blessed are the meek, for they will inherit the earth." |

The meek, in English usage, includes those who are not violent or strong and those who endure injury with patience and without resentment. Obviously membership in this population is no more popular today than it was in Jesus' time. But the promise is still as attractive.

| Matt. 5: 6 "Blessed are those who hunger and thirst for righteousness, for they will be filled." | Luke 6: 21 "Blessed are you who are hungry now, for you will be filled." |

Hungering and thirsting for righteousness (or justice) demands a sacrifice of our own self-interest and our own self-conceits. This was never a popular concept even when performed to build a stronger relationship with the creator god.

| Matt. 5: 7 "Blessed are the merciful, for they will receive mercy." |

To be merciful demands that we not take advantage of our superior strengths to force our will on others, and that we help those who are less fortunate than we are.

> Matt. 5: 8 "Blessed are the pure in heart, for they will see God."

This purity demands a surrender of our own desires and lusts when they come between us and other people or between us and God.

> Matt. 5: 9 "Blessed are the peacemakers, for they will be called children of God."

Jesus continues with promises of blessings for all manner of men who have no wealth or power, men who are forgiving and not aggressive. These are men striving to bring others together in peace and willing to make peace even if that requires sacrifice.

| Matt. 5: 10 "Blessed are those who are persecuted for righteousness' sake, for theirs is the kingdom of heaven.
11 "Blessed are you when people revile you and persecute you and utter all kinds of evil against you falsely on my account.
12 Rejoice and be glad, for your reward is great in heaven, for in the same way they persecuted the prophets who were before you." | Luke 6: 22 "Blessed are you when people hate you, and when they exclude you, revile you, and defame you on account of the Son of Man.
23 Rejoice in that day and leap for joy, for surely your reward is great in heaven; for that is what their ancestors did to the prophets." |

> John 15: 18 "If the world hates you, be aware that it hated me before it hated you.
> 19 If you belonged to the world, the world would love you as its own. Because you do not belong to the world, but I have chosen you out of the world--therefore the world hates you."

Jesus tells his followers to expect hatred and persecution from those who pretend to be God's followers but who worship worldly things. There have been times when the Roman Church, the Gnostics, protestants, Mormons and Jehovah's Witnesses, among others, have experienced this hatred and persecution. Certainly no mainstream group suffers it today.

> Luke 6: 24 "But woe to you who are rich, for you have received your consolation.
> 25 "Woe to you who are full now, for you will be hungry. Woe to you who are laughing now, for you will mourn and weep.
> 26 Woe to you when all speak well of you, for that is what their ancestors did to the false prophets."

In Luke, Jesus follows the other beatitudes with the promises to those who prosper in this world. The substance of the message is that Christians should expect god's reward in heaven rather than in this life. We cannot have it both ways. These promises are so unattractive (and appeal to such unattractive people, as they did in Jesus' day) that they are seldom mentioned in the modern church.

Despite all the currently popular promises about worldly wealth and power and pleasure and popularity for church members, Jesus makes it clear here, and in other places, that such blessings have little or nothing to do with his kingdom. The same is true for those who put other treasures ahead of the creator god's will.

The apostles, Stephen, and the Roman martyrs were apparently able to believe this promise (though history teaches us that many members of the church in Rome recanted their faith to avoid persecution). In later years church members have often preferred to face their enemies with swords and rifles rather than with forgiveness, prayers and hymns. (It's often tempting to defend democracy or freedom or capitalism in the name of defending Christianity.)

Some churches today may expect that their foreign missionaries might go into harm's way on occasion. (I know of one instance where the Mormons withdrew some missionaries from a Southern community because some locals were so hostile.) But no 'First Church' of any denomination in any American city lives with the clouds of religious persecution hanging over the congregation's heads on a daily basis. This, of course, raises the question of whether we deserve the rewards Jesus promises.

The Law

> Matt. 5: 17 "Do not think that I have come to abolish the law or the prophets; I have come not to abolish but to fulfill.
> 18 For truly I tell you, until heaven and earth pass away, not one letter, not one stroke of a letter, will pass from the law until all is accomplished.
> 19 Therefore, whoever breaks one of the least of these commandments, and teaches others to do the same, will be called least in the kingdom of heaven; but whoever does them and teaches them will be called great in the kingdom of heaven.
> 20 For I tell you, unless your righteousness exceeds that of the scribes and Pharisees, you will never enter the kingdom of heaven."

Surely Jesus referred to the ten commandments and his distillation of them into two. The average American church member would be hard pressed to list all ten of the commandments much less to obey them. Jesus' behavior suggests he did not hold the Old Testament dietary laws, and reams of other regulations levied on the people by their religious leaders, in equally high regard. He surely didn't seem to endorse the stoning of disobedient sons[4] or prostitutes[5] and many other punishments prescribed in the first five books of the Old Testament. Nor did he seem to worry that the Jews had stolen the Holy Land from its historic owners, slaughtered opponents from the day Moses came down from the mountain, and committed adultery at least from the days of King David.

By his actions and teachings Jesus sought to expand or reveal how the creator god's laws were to be lived out by his followers.

> Matt. 5: 21 "You have heard that it was said to those of ancient times, 'You shall not murder'; and 'whoever murders shall be liable to judgment.'
> 22 But I say to you that if you are angry with a brother or sister, you will be liable to judgment; and if you insult a brother or sister, you will be liable to the council; and if you say, 'You fool,' you will be liable to the hell of fire.
> 23 So when you are offering your gift at the altar, if you remember that your brother or sister has something against you,
> 24 leave your gift there before the altar and go; first be reconciled to your brother or sister, and then come and offer your gift."

Again, Jesus identifies self-control and humility as necessary qualities of life for his followers. He makes anger as sinful as murder. And he teaches that the principles of the law are more important than the nitty gritty particulars. It seems likely that he would have given the terms 'brother' and 'sister' interpretations as broad as the one he gave 'neighbor' in the parable of the good Samaritan.

	Luke 12: 57 "And why do you not judge for yourselves what is right?
Matt. 5: 25 "Come to terms	58 Thus, when you go with

---

[4] Deut. 21: 18-21
[5] Deut. 22: 20-21

quickly with your accuser while you are on the way to court with him, or your accuser may hand you over to the judge, and the judge to the guard, and you will be thrown into prison. 26 Truly I tell you, you will never get out until you have paid the last penny."	your accuser before a magistrate, on the way make an effort to settle the case, or you may be dragged before the judge, and the judge hand you over to the officer, and the officer throw you in prison. 59 I tell you, you will never get out until you have paid the very last penny."

And he extends his demands for peacemaking even to everyday life and disagreements among friends, relatives and even neighbors and enemies.

> Matt. 5: 27 "You have heard that it was said, 'You shall not commit adultery.'
> 28 But I say to you that everyone who looks at a woman with lust has already committed adultery with her in his heart."

Jesus elevated lust to the same level of sinfulness as adultery, but America has made adultery and divorce and pornography, even without repentance, forgivable if not socially acceptable.

Matt. 5: 9 "And if your eye causes you to stumble, tear it out and throw it away; it is better for you to enter life with one eye than to have two eyes and to be thrown into the hell of fire." Matt. 5: 29 "If your right eye causes you to sin, tear it out	Mark 9: 47 "And if your eye causes you to stumble, tear it out; it is better for you to enter the kingdom of God with one eye than to have two eyes and to be thrown into hell, 48 where their worm never dies, and the fire is never quenched."

and throw it away; it is better for you to lose one of your members than for your whole body to be thrown into hell."	
Matt. 5: 30 "And if your right hand causes you to sin, cut it off and throw it away; it is better for you to lose one of your members than for your whole body to go into hell."	Mark 9: 43 "If your hand causes you to stumble, cut it off; it is better for you to enter life maimed than to have two hands and to go to hell, to the unquenchable fire."
Matt. 18: 8 "If your hand or your foot causes you to stumble, cut it off and throw it away; it is better for you to enter life maimed or lame than to have two hands or two feet and to be thrown into the eternal fire."	Mark 9: 45 "And if your foot causes you to stumble, cut it off; it is better for you to enter life lame than to have two feet and to be thrown into hell."

We would like to believe Jesus wasn't really suggesting we tear out an eye or cut off a hand. But he was surely teaching that even valuable or important or cherished elements of our lives and our thinking should be sacrificed rather than let them drag us into Hell. Surely possessions and power are as important to some people as a hand or a foot.

Jesus spoke often of punishment for sinners after their deaths. He talked of 'outer darkness,' 'gnashing of teeth,' and Hell. But Satan has managed to remove Hell from the vocabulary of many main-stream church members. The concept of punishment after the death of this body is far from the mind of many financially comfortable church members. Certainly, fear of Hell is not a popular recruiting tool for the Prosperity Gospel and 'Christianity is fun' churches.

Divorce and Adultery

| Matt. 5: 31 "It was also said, 'Whoever divorces his wife, let him give her a certificate of divorce.' 32 But I say to you that anyone who divorces his wife, except on the ground of unchastity, causes her to commit adultery; and whoever marries a divorced woman commits adultery."

 Matt. 19: 9 "And I say to you, whoever divorces his wife, except for unchastity, and marries another commits adultery." | Mark 10: 11 He said to them, "Whoever divorces his wife and marries another commits adultery against her; 12 and if she divorces her husband and marries another, she commits adultery." | Luke 16: 18 "Anyone who divorces his wife and marries another commits adultery,

 and whoever marries a woman divorced from her husband commits adultery." |

    Jesus obviously held marriage in higher regard than American society does today. The prohibitions on adultery and divorce are both popular topics for situational ethics, which readily explains them as being intended for someone else in another time and different circumstances.

    I think it's revealing that so many 'good church members' can strain at the 'gnat' of homosexuality (which Jesus didn't mention) while ignoring the 'log' of adultery and divorce (which

Jesus condemned harshly). He even prescribed celibacy as appropriate behavior for divorced people. But his prescription of celibacy 'does not preach' in most modern churches.

Oaths

> Matt. 5: 33 "Again, you have heard that it was said to those of ancient times, 'You shall not swear falsely, but carry out the vows you have made to the Lord.'
> 34 But I say to you, Do not swear at all, either by heaven, for it is the throne of God,
> 35 or by the earth, for it is his footstool, or by Jerusalem, for it is the city of the great King.
> 36 And do not swear by your head, for you cannot make one hair white or black.
> 37 Let your word be 'Yes, Yes' or 'No, No'; anything more than this comes from the evil one."

Obviously this is contrary to the longstanding (and essentially meaningless) practice of taking oaths on the Bible in courts and oaths of office in political settings. The demand of course is for personal integrity in the sight of God.

Behavior/Relationship

Matt. 5: 38 "You have heard that it was said, 'An eye for an eye and a tooth for a tooth.' 39 But I say to you, Do not resist an evildoer. But if anyone strikes you on the right cheek, turn the other also; 40 and if anyone wants to sue you and take your coat, give your cloak as well; 41 and if anyone forces you to	Luke 6: 29 "If anyone strikes you on the cheek, offer the other also; and from anyone who takes away your coat do not withhold even your shirt."

go one mile, go also the second mile."	

Here Jesus contradicts the Old Testament teachings and the popular practice of 'an eye for an eye and a tooth for a tooth.' Obviously he was calling his followers to a radically higher (if unpopular) standard of behavior in dealing with those Jewish rulers and the Romans who victimized the poor.

Many scholars believe the Greek that is here translated as 'resist' is better translated as 'resist with violence.' This same sort of non-violent resistance (though based on The Upanishads) worked well for Mahatma Gandhi, Martin Luther King, Jr. and others. The standard is as unpopular today (even in the church) as it was in Jesus' day.

Matt. 5: 42 "Give to everyone who begs from you, and do not refuse anyone who wants to borrow from you."	Luke 6: 30 "Give to everyone who begs from you; and if anyone takes away your goods, do not ask for them again."

In this teaching, which is obviously and painfully contrary to normal self-interest, Jesus is telling his followers to put their faith in God rather than in money and other 'stuff.'

One has only to consider the poor populations in this country and the world (in the midst of the churches' opulence) to see how we ignore this lesson or depend on the various governments and charitable organizations to express God's love in our stead. In effect, modern churches have promoted various governments to the status of God for the poor and disadvantaged.

Matt. 5: 43 "You have heard that it was said, 'You shall love your neighbor and hate your enemy.' 44 But I say to you, Love your	Luke 6: 27 "But I say to you that

enemies and pray for those who persecute you, 45 so that you may be children of your Father in heaven; for he makes his sun rise on the evil and on the good, and sends rain on the righteous and on the unrighteous. 46 For if you love those who love you, what reward do you have? Do not even the tax collectors do the same? 47 And if you greet only your brothers and sisters, what more are you doing than others? Do not even the Gentiles do the same? 48 Be perfect, therefore, as your heavenly Father is perfect."	listen, Love your enemies, do good to those who hate you, 28 bless those who curse you, pray for those who abuse you. Luke 6: 32 "If you love those who love you, what credit is that to you? For even sinners love those who love them. 33 If you do good to those who do good to you, what credit is that to you? For even sinners do the same. 34 If you lend to those from whom you hope to receive, what credit is that to you? Even sinners lend to sinners, to receive as much again. 35 But love your enemies, do good, and lend, expecting nothing in return. Your reward will be great, and you will be children of the Most High; for he is kind to the ungrateful and the wicked. 36 Be merciful, just as your Father is merciful."

    While this is completely consistent with Jesus' teachings, nothing could be more opposed to normal self-interest and nothing could be more unpopular with men and women who put their trust and their efforts into accumulating and enjoying the power and riches and comforts of this world.

Unfortunately, many churches lavish their love on members of their 'church family' and avoid anyone who is less loveable because of race, nationality or social class.

I don't recall ever hearing a 'Christian,' in a church or any other public place, pray for the Nazi or Japanese enemies, the North Korean or North Vietnamese enemies, or the Al-Qaeda and other current terrorist enemies. But Jesus seems to be telling us to do so.

In effect, Jesus calls on his followers to be as loving as God is. If churches started insisting on this behavior from their leaders and members many congregations would wither on the vine. And others would show the world a whole new religion.

> Matt. 6: 1 "Beware of practicing your piety before others in order to be seen by them; for then you have no reward from your Father in heaven.
> 2 So whenever you give alms, do not sound a trumpet before you, as the hypocrites do in the synagogues and in the streets, so that they may be praised by others. Truly I tell you, they have received their reward.
> 3 But when you give alms, do not let your left hand know what your right hand is doing,
> 4 so that your alms may be done in secret; and your Father who sees in secret will reward you."

All of us would enjoy being praised and recognized for our contributions to the church, in time, effort and money. This passage warns us to be careful of our motives and to look for our praise from God rather than from men. It also raises serious questions about the practice of asking members to make pledges for the support of the church and its programs and plant. And, of course, the purpose of alms was not to build buildings but to minister to the poor.

(See also The Golden Rule: p. 67.)

Prayer

> Matt. 6: 5 "And whenever you pray, do not be like the hypocrites; for they love to stand and pray in the synagogues and at the street corners, so that they may be seen by others. Truly I tell you, they have received their reward.
> 6 But whenever you pray, go into your room and shut the door and pray to your Father who is in secret; and your Father who sees in secret will reward you.
> 7 When you are praying, do not heap up empty phrases as the Gentiles do; for they think that they will be heard because of their many words.
> 8 Do not be like them, for your Father knows what you need before you ask him."

Here we find a whole new, and easily forgotten, perspective on worship. We learn, if we have eyes to see, that private worship is much more attractive to God than grandiose public rituals, elaborate entertainment and pretentious prayers.

In many of today's churches the practices of solitude and silence are almost non-existent. Every minute of worship must be filled with words and/or music. And for many congregations it's a sin to run the Sabbath service longer than an hour.

Surely anyone who has suffered through a seemingly endless pastoral prayer is entitled to wonder if the pastor has ever read this passage.

The passage also reminds us to trust God and depend on him for the things we need each day.

The Lord's Prayer

| Matt. 6: 9 "Pray then in this way: Our Father in heaven, | Luke 11: 2 He said to them, "When you pray, say: Father, |

| hallowed be your name. | hallowed be your name. |

This salutation is more than an act of respect for God. It is a claim on relationship with the creator. And, at the same time, it goes beyond the family and the congregation. It is a recognition of our relationship with all men.

| Matt. 6: 10 "Your kingdom come. Your will be done, on earth as it is in heaven. | "Your kingdom come. |

Obviously, the doing of God's will starts in the hearts and minds of those who believe Jesus. Jesus tells us to surrender our wills to God's will and to do our part in making his kingdom a reality on earth. He even tells followers that the kingdom of God is within or among them.[6]

Men and women in today's world show very little of the appetite for God's kingdom that the Roman martyrs showed. Only the prospect of reuniting with loved ones seems to get much of our attention. Many church members have only a vague, romantic or 'glorious' concept of heaven. And even that is not appealing enough to make us eager or ready to pay the price.

| Matt. 6: 11 "Give us this day our daily bread. | Luke 11: 3 "Give us each day our daily bread. |

Here, and in other places, Jesus encourages us to be completely surrendered to God and dependent on him not only for food and protection and forgiveness, but for the presence of Jesus in our lives on a daily basis.

It's worth noting that Jesus did not tell his audience to ask God 'to help them get' their daily bread. As he taught in Matthew

---

[6] Luke 17: 21.

6: 25-34, he encourages his followers to expect God's provision on a day-to-day basis.

| Matt 6: 12 "And forgive us our debts, as we also have forgiven our debtors. | Luke 11: 4 "And forgive us our sins, for we ourselves forgive everyone indebted to us. |

In effect, Jesus teaches us to pray that God will love us and forgive us exactly as much as we love and forgive our worst enemies and debtors.

| Matt 6: 13 "And do not bring us to the time of trial, but rescue us from the evil one." | "And do not bring us to the time of trial." |

Again, the prayer is a prayer of surrender and dependence on God's will. It is also a confirmation that Jesus believed in the reality of Satan.

It's worth noting that the prayer is a daily prayer of surrender, not a weekly exercise of ritual.

Write down how your daily surrender could be accomplished and what the benefits would be.

Write down how 'the evil one' tempts you.

Forgiveness

| Matt. 6: 14 "For if you forgive others their trespasses, your heavenly Father will also forgive you; 15 but if you do not forgive others, neither will your Father forgive your trespasses." | Mark 11: 25 "Whenever you stand praying, forgive, if you have anything against anyone; so that your Father in heaven may also forgive you your trespasses." |

Some churches make a fuss about the use of 'debts' or 'trespasses' or 'sins' in this prayer. God doesn't care. He's only concerned about your relationship with his other children. Jesus makes the receipt of God's forgiveness conditional on our own forgiving. He teaches us to practice a level of forgiveness in our daily lives that is sometimes hard to discern in today's 'Christian' community.

Fasting

> Matt. 6: 16 "And whenever you fast, do not look dismal, like the hypocrites, for they disfigure their faces so as to show others that they are fasting. Truly I tell you, they have received their reward. 17 But when you fast, put oil on your head and wash your face, 18 so that your fasting may be seen not by others but by your Father who is in secret; and your Father who sees in secret will reward you."

It's hard to identify a denomination with a meaningful doctrine regarding fasting in overfed America. The sacrifices we make voluntarily are almost imperceptible. This may be good if that is the intention, but it's not so good if the sacrifices are non-existent.

Treasures on Earth

Matt. 6: 19 "Do not store up for yourselves treasures on earth, where moth and rust consume and where thieves break in and steal;	
20 but store up for yourselves treasures in heaven, where	Luke 12: 33 "Sell your possessions, and give alms.

neither moth nor rust consumes and where thieves do not break in and steal. 21 For where your treasure is, there your heart will be also."	Make purses for yourselves that do not wear out, an unfailing treasure in heaven, where no thief comes near and no moth destroys. 34 For where your treasure is, there your heart will be also." Luke 14: 33 "So therefore, none of you can become my disciple if you do not give up all your possessions."

The whole concept of the so-called 'Prosperity Gospel' and the longstanding practice of main-stream and fundamentalist churches in modern America contradicts this and other of Jesus' teachings. They tend to ignore the suffering of generations of followers, and seem to adhere to some Old Testament passages that attribute great wealth to being in God's favor.

Most modern church members would certainly consider the 'holy poverty' of the disciples and other revered leaders, such as St. Francis, to be unnecessary aberrations. We are so spoiled to our everyday affluence that we have convinced ourselves that we deserve all the riches we enjoy. And we somehow believe that what we have is not enough.

The problem with possessions, obviously, is that we become dependent on them and let them become a barrier between God and us and between us and our fellow men. (Just as happened with the church in Europe during the Nazi reign, and with the church in America's South for more than 200 years.) Churches and their members sell their Christian principles to save their property. Many congregations and priests/ministers are more preoccupied with the prosperity and comfort of the church than they are with the god of the church or with the poor in their communities. Too many church members believe that stained glass windows, air conditioning and elaborate show-business worship productions somehow glorify the creator god.

In the meantime, 'the church' builds bigger and more self-aggrandizing mausoleums, complete with stained glass windows and rock bands. And it ignores the ravaged peoples of Rwanda and Darfur ("But we need a new family center for the congregation."). 'The church' can't even minister to the 12 million homeless children in the U. S. A. ("The government will take care of them. But don't raise our taxes.")

The Lamp of the Body

| Matt. 6: 22 "The eye is the lamp of the body. So, if your eye is healthy, your whole body will be full of light; 23 but if your eye is unhealthy, your whole body will be full of darkness. If then the light in you is darkness, how great is the darkness!" | Luke 11: 34 "Your eye is the lamp of your body. If your eye is healthy, your whole body is full of light; but if it is not healthy, your body is full of darkness. 35 Therefore consider whether the light in you is not darkness. 36 If then your whole body is full of light, with no part of it in darkness, it will be as full of light as when a lamp gives you light with its rays." |

Jesus teaches us that we should keep our attention on God's desires for our lives and let those desires enlighten us. Lust and covetousness and pride can easily lead us astray and condemn us.

Two Masters

Matt. 6: 24 "No one can serve two masters; for a slave will either hate the one and love the other, or be devoted to the one and despise the other. You cannot serve God and wealth."	Luke 16: 13 "No slave can serve two masters; for a slave will either hate the one and love the other, or be devoted to the one and despise the other. You cannot serve God and wealth."

The passages make it clear that we cannot devote our time and attention exclusively to the pursuit of wealth and still be faithful to the creator god. Many ministries have denied this (and do so today) on the basis of one or two verses that talk about abundance as if it were promised to all believers in this life.

Be aware that 'the church' cannot change this situation.

- It is too committed to bigger buildings and bigger mortgages.
- It is too committed to elaborate perks for the church bureaucracy.
- It is too committed to a prestigious place in the community.
- It is too reluctant to suffer or experience discomfort or unpopularity.

Only you, with the help of the Holy Spirit, can shape your life in accord with this teaching. Only you, with the help of the Holy Spirit, can reshape your congregation so that it glorifies God in keeping with his teachings.

Depend on God

Matt. 6: 25 "Therefore I tell you,	Luke 12: 22 He said to his disciples, "Therefore I tell you,

do not worry about your life, what you will eat or what you will drink, or about your body, what you will wear. Is not life more than food, and the body more than clothing? 26 Look at the birds of the air; they neither sow nor reap nor gather into barns, and yet your heavenly Father feeds them. Are you not of more value than they? 27 And can any of you by worrying add a single hour to your span of life? 28 And why do you worry about clothing? Consider the lilies of the field, how they grow; they neither toil nor spin, 29 yet I tell you, even Solomon in all his glory was not clothed like one of these. 30 But if God so clothes the grass of the field, which is alive today and tomorrow is thrown into the oven, will he not much more clothe you--you of little faith? 31 Therefore do not worry, saying, 'What will we eat?' or 'What will we drink?' or 'What will we wear?' 32 For it is the Gentiles who strive for all these things; and indeed your heavenly Father	do not worry about your life, what you will eat, or about your body, what you will wear. 23 For life is more than food, and the body more than clothing. 24 Consider the ravens: they neither sow nor reap, they have neither storehouse nor barn, and yet God feeds them. Of how much more value are you than the birds! 25 And can any of you by worrying add a single hour to your span of life? 26 If then you are not able to do so small a thing as that, why do you worry about the rest? 27 Consider the lilies, how they grow: they neither toil nor spin; yet I tell you, even Solomon in all his glory was not clothed like one of these. 28 But if God so clothes the grass of the field, which is alive today and tomorrow is thrown into the oven, how much more will he clothe you--you of little faith! 29 And do not keep striving for what you are to eat and what you are to drink, and do not keep worrying. 30 For it is the nations of the world that strive after all these things, and your Father knows

knows that you need all these things." 33 But strive first for the kingdom of God and his righteousness, and all these things will be given to you as well. 34 "So do not worry about tomorrow, for tomorrow will bring worries of its own. Today's trouble is enough for today."	that you need them. 31 Instead, strive for his kingdom, and these things will be given to you as well."

Here is one of those teachings even the most fundamentalist denominations treat as totally impractical, no matter how much we might wish it were not.

Paul and some of the disciples apparently practiced the teaching at times. And the church in Jerusalem seems to have followed the basic tenet for a while. But the communism and dependence on God which that church practiced have been unacceptable to most denominations for centuries. It will probably be thus so long as we look for treasures in this world rather than in heaven.

Like many of Jesus' other teachings this one is often explained away or ignored as having 'expired' or having been intended for a very select audience. Even most monastic orders don't seem to take it seriously.

Matt. 7: 1 "Do not judge, so that you may not be judged. 2 For with the judgment you make you will be judged, and the measure you give will be the measure you get.	Luke 6: 37 "Do not judge, and you will not be judged; do not condemn, and you will not be condemned. Forgive, and you will be forgiven; 38 give, and it will be given to you. A good measure, pressed down, shaken together, running over, will be put into your lap;

	for the measure you give will be the measure you get back."
3 Why do you see the speck in your neighbor's eye, but do not notice the log in your own eye?	Luke 6: 41 Why do you see the speck in your neighbor's eye, but do not notice the log in your own eye?
4 Or how can you say to your neighbor, 'Let me take the speck out of your eye,' while the log is in your own eye?	42 Or how can you say to your neighbor, 'Friend, let me take out the speck in your eye,' when you yourself do not see the log in your own eye? You hypocrite, first take the log out of your own eye, and then you will see clearly to take the speck out of your neighbor's eye."
5 You hypocrite, first take the log out of your own eye, and then you will see clearly to take the speck out of your neighbor's eye."	

And, again, he promises that we will receive our reward in heaven if we live the kind of life he prescribes.

This forbearance and humility is as radical as many of Jesus' other teachings, even within our churches. Jesus excuses us from any responsibility for making judgements or exacting revenge on our fellow men. Instead, he expects us to forgive our fellow men as we would like God to forgive our debts and trespasses.

Our society is anchored on the making of judgements. And our churches often pride themselves on being 'better than' their neighbors.

Matt. 7: 6 "Do not give what is holy to dogs; and do not throw your pearls before swine, or they will trample them under foot and turn and maul you."

Jesus warned his followers to share the treasures of the kingdom only with those who were open to accept them and not to invite attack by presenting his secrets to those who would respond viciously. (Indeed, he used parables to avoid the reproach of some of those he criticized most harshly.)

Some of today's churches, in order to win popularity, don't present the secrets at all. Instead they offer fellowship, comfort, positive thinking, and entertainment in a variety of forms, to give their members a 'good' feeling about themselves. And those churches never confront their members with the responsibilities and sacrifices that Jesus' demands.

Matt. 7: 7 "Ask, and it will be given you; search, and you will find; knock, and the door will be opened for you. 8 For everyone who asks receives, and everyone who searches finds, and for everyone who knocks, the door will be opened. 9 Is there anyone among you who, if your child asks for bread, will give a stone? 10 Or if the child asks for a fish, will give a snake?	Luke 11: 9 "So I say to you, Ask, and it will be given you; search, and you will find; knock, and the door will be opened for you. 10 For everyone who asks receives, and everyone who searches finds, and for everyone who knocks, the door will be opened. 11 Is there anyone among you who, if your child asks for a fish, will give a snake instead of a fish? 12 Or if the child asks for an egg, will give a scorpion?
11 If you then, who are evil, know how to give good gifts to your children, how much more will your Father in heaven give good things to those who ask him!"	13 If you then, who are evil, know how to give good gifts to your children, how much more will the heavenly Father give the Holy Spirit to those who ask him!"

One of the hardest of Jesus' lessons, this teaching calls on believers to be completely surrendered to the creator god and completely trusting and dependent on him for all their needs. Luke's account also presents the intriguing idea that the Holy Spirit is a gift, not to everyone who joins a church, but to those who ask the creator god by doing his will.

Almost no modern churches seem to take the promises seriously. Certainly, the teachings fly in the face of Paul's example and the 'Puritan work ethic.' Cessationists would surely say the promises were limited to a few people for a short period of time and that the promises expired long ago. Most people, including many church leaders, would blame the failures of the promises on 'God's will.'

This teaching also flies in the face of the popular modern heresy that "God helps those who help themselves."[7]

But, if we can't believe Jesus about these promises, how can we believe his promises of eternal life and heaven?

The Golden Rule

| Matt. 7: 12 "In everything do to others as you would have them do to you; for this is the law and the prophets." | Luke 6: 31 "Do to others as you would have them do to you." |

Another of Jesus' harder teachings, this is the so-called 'Golden Rule.' While many of the world's religions have similar teachings only a couple of them call on the practitioner to be as proactive as Jesus does. When required to justify war or slavery or the theft of other peoples' lands, most 'Christians' rely on passages from the Old Testament to salve their consciences. Some even find passages that serve to justify our lust and our lack of compassion.

---

[7] Popularized and/or invented by Ben Franklin.

> Luke 6: 27 "But I say to you that listen, Love your enemies, do good to those who hate you,
> 28 bless those who curse you, pray for those who abuse you.
> 29 If anyone strikes you on the cheek, offer the other also; and from anyone who takes away your coat do not withhold even your shirt.
> 30 Give to everyone who begs from you; and if anyone takes away your goods, do not ask for them again."

Then Jesus proceeds to give his followers a set of radical examples to follow if they want to find favor with the creator god.

What we ignore is the fact that this 'Golden Rule' requires us to live our lives in a proactive mode: to **do** positive, loving things for a multitude of people (our neighbors), not just to refrain from doing negative things. It also requires that we give serious thought to what sort of things we would want others to do to/for us consistent with God's will. And, for those who are born again Christians, this includes sharing Jesus with others: the one thing we can do that sinners or mere pretenders cannot do.

> John 15: 12 "This is my commandment, that you love one another as I have loved you.
> 13 No one has greater love than this, to lay down one's life for one's friends.
> 14 You are my friends if you do what I command you."

The guidelines are so contrary to our natural self-interests that Jesus points out the contrast between his rules and the rules of common sense survival in the world of his day (and of our day).

He also points out that following his commandments is mandatory for those wanting to 'be his friend.'

Ask yourself how you can do a better job of practicing 'The Golden Rule."

(See also Behavior/Relationship: p. 52)

The Narrow Gate

Matt. 7: 13 "Enter through the narrow gate; for the gate is wide and the road is easy that leads to destruction, and there are many who take it. 14 For the gate is narrow and the road is hard that leads to life, and there are few who find it."	Luke 13: 23 Someone asked him, "Lord, will only a few be saved?" He said to them, 24 "Strive to enter through the narrow door; for many, I tell you, will try to enter and will not be able."

Here and in other places, Jesus made it perfectly clear that eternal life is not for everyone. And he promises that the path is not easy, even for believers.

Unfortunately, many churches, in their lust for popularity and power and wealth, have ignored or watered down this teaching. They have encouraged members to believe that goodness or niceness, and lip service to Jesus and devotion to the church are what is required to reach Heaven. And they often teach that this behavior, even without sacrifice or repentance, promises followers an abundance of worldly goods in this life.

If you have persuaded yourself that following Jesus is easy and popular and fun, your soul may be in great danger. And if you avoid sharing Jesus, in word and deed, with others because it may earn you criticism or because it may be 'politically incorrect' your soul may be in great danger.

The Saved and the Damned

Jesus makes it clear that not everyone who 'believes in' him will enter his kingdom. Even Satan and the demons believed in Jesus. Even religious leaders may be cast out if they ignore his demands.

Matt. 7: 21 "Not everyone who says to me, 'Lord, Lord,' will enter the kingdom of heaven, but only the one who does the will of my Father in heaven. 22 On that day many will say to me, 'Lord, Lord, did we not prophesy in your name, and cast out demons in your name, and do many deeds of power in your name?' 23 Then I will declare to them, 'I never knew you; go away from me, you evildoers.'"	Luke 6: 46 "Why do you call me 'Lord, Lord,' and do not what I tell you? Luke 13: 26 Then you will begin to say, 'We ate and drank with you, and you taught in our streets.' 27 But he will say, 'I do not know where you come from; go away from me, all you evildoers!' 28 There will be weeping and gnashing of teeth when you see Abraham and Isaac and Jacob and all the prophets in the kingdom of God, and you yourselves thrown out."

This is the crux of our judgement: no matter how loudly we sing; no matter how fervently we pray; no matter how much time and money we give to the church; no matter how many nice things we do for our friends and neighbors; we will be cast out of his kingdom unless we do God's will.

Unfortunately many church members have little or no understanding of what 'doing God's will' amounts to.[8]

Matt. 7: 24 "Everyone then who hears these words of mine and acts on them will be like a wise man who built his house on rock. 25 The rain fell, the floods came, and the winds blew and beat on that house, but it did not fall, because it had been founded on rock. 26 And everyone who hears these words of mine and does not act on them will be like a foolish man who built his house on sand. 27 The rain fell, and the floods came, and the winds blew and beat against that house, and it fell--and great was its fall!"	Luke 6: 47 "I will show you what someone is like who comes to me, hears my words, and acts on them. 48 That one is like a man building a house, who dug deeply and laid the foundation on rock; when a flood arose, the river burst against that house but could not shake it, because it had been well built. 49 But the one who hears and does not act is like a man who built a house on the ground without a foundation. When the river burst against it, immediately it fell, and great was the ruin of that house."

This parable tells us again that believing is without merit unless we act on our beliefs.

The parable can be especially threatening to pastors and other church leaders who preach comfort and popularity and power instead of suffering and sacrifice and surrender.

Good Fruit/Bad Fruit

Matt. 7: 15 "Beware of false	

---

[8] For a discussion of God's revealed will see Appendix II.

prophets, who come to you in sheep's clothing but inwardly are ravenous wolves. 16 You will know them by their fruits. Are grapes gathered from thorns, or figs from thistles? 17 In the same way, every good tree bears good fruit, but the bad tree bears bad fruit. 18 A good tree cannot bear bad fruit, nor can a bad tree bear good fruit. 19 Every tree that does not bear good fruit is cut down and thrown into the fire. Thus you will know them by their fruits." Matt. 3: 10 "Even now the ax is lying at the root of the trees; every tree therefore that does not bear good fruit is cut down and thrown into the fire." Matt. 12: 33 "Either make the tree good, and its fruit good; or make the tree bad, and its fruit bad; for the tree is known by its fruit. 34 You brood of vipers! How can you speak good things, when you are evil? For out of the abundance of the heart the mouth speaks. 35 The good person brings	Luke 6: 44 "for each tree is known by its own fruit. Figs are not gathered from thorns, nor are grapes picked from a bramble bush." Luke 6: 43 "No good tree bears bad fruit, nor again does a bad tree bear good fruit;" 45 "The good person out of

good things out of a good treasure, and the evil person brings evil things out of an evil treasure. "	the good treasure of the heart produces good, and the evil person out of evil treasure produces evil; for it is out of the abundance of the heart that the mouth speaks."

This teaching is most threatening to church leaders who seek power and prestige and popularity ahead of surrender to God and dependence on him.

No one can argue that American churches are not filled with 'good people' and 'nice people' doing nice things and good things for their families and church friends and even their neighbors. But even the tax collectors of Jesus' time did nice things and good things for their families and friends.

Jesus might question whether spending millions of dollars on church buildings for the comfort and convenience and recreation of the members is 'bearing good fruit.' This is especially problematic when millions of people in the world are in desperate need of food and water and shelter.

It seems the churches of America would be embarrassed by the fact that Bill Gates, Warren Buffett, and Oprah Winfrey and many show business figures are giving more assistance to the poor and oppressed in Africa than American churches have done over centuries. Even the entertainment community seems to be more interested in humanitarian causes than 'the church' is.

Other Forgotten Parables

Some of Jesus' teachings are reported in only one of the synoptic gospels. Some are reported in more than one gospel. Many of them are presented in simple stories called parables and in one liners called aphorisms. Jesus said he preferred to use parables so that his critics and the indifferent among his listeners would not understand them.[9] Sometimes even his twelve disciples needed to have a parable explained. He made it clear that he expected many who heard him to reject his teachings.[10] He also anticipated that many of his followers would desert him when the going got tough. Some of the lessons are presented in more than one parable using slightly different imagery.

In any case, many of the parables might be thought of as illustrations of God's will in action among men. In his book *Jesus*, Borg reminds us that the parables aren't just good stories. They "invite the audience to make a judgment. Implicitly, the parables begin or end with, 'What do you think?'" They provoke discussion. They invite us to see things differently. Ideally they prompt church members to act differently from non-members.

I don't think there's any magic way to sort the parables. Bible scholars seem to differ on what they consider a parable, so the numbers differ from writer to writer. Feel free to sort them any way you like. That's not the important thing anyway. What you need to consider is what they teach and how well you are shaping your life in response to that teaching.

---

[9] Matt. 13: 13-14.
[10] Matt. 15: 15.

For this prophecy I've chosen some groupings that I find helpful.

Love, Trust and Obey God

The foundation for Christianity (and the Jewish religion) is trust in the creator god and love (honor, respect, and obedience) for him. The essence of sin is self-centerdness and self-reliance. Jesus taught that the creator god offers eternal life for those who put him first in their lives. It was radical then and it is radical now. He also promised believers that God will provide for their daily needs.

One element that gives Christianity value is that God lets each of us choose whether we will trust and obey him or not. The price of relationship with the creator god (and our fellow men) includes putting others' interests ahead of our own and trusting God. Most conventional men/women find the price too high to pay. We find it almost impossible to act as if the god who fed and clothed 400,000+ people in the wilderness for forty years can provide for our daily needs.

Matt. 10: 34 "Do not think that I have come to bring peace to the earth; I have not come to bring peace, but a sword. 35 For I have come to set a man against his father, and a daughter against her mother, and a daughter-in-law against her mother-in-law; 36 and one's foes will be members of one's own household. 37 Whoever loves father or mother more than me is not worthy of me; and whoever	Luke 14: 26 "Whoever comes to me and does not hate father and mother, wife and children, brothers and sisters, yes, and even life itself, cannot be my disciple."

| loves son or daughter more than me is not worthy of me;" | |

Jesus' teachings flew in the face of the conventional paternalistic society of the Jews. This teaching warned the Jews that they must love Jesus' new teachings more than those of the clutter of regulations imposed on them by their religious leaders.

No part of Jesus' ministry was more important to him (and to us) than his focus on building man's relationship with the creator god. Most of the people of his time, both Jews and Gentiles, chose to ignore his message just as most people, church members and others, ignore the message today. Love, trust and obedience are integral to our part in that relationship. Blessings, salvation, forgiveness and love are aspects of God's side of the relationship.

| Matt. 10: 32 "Everyone therefore who acknowledges me before others, I also will acknowledge before my Father in heaven; 33 but whoever denies me before others, I also will deny before my Father in heaven." | Mark 8: 38 "Those who are ashamed of me and of my words in this adulterous and sinful generation, of them the Son of Man will also be ashamed when he comes in the glory of his Father with the holy angels." | Luke 9: 26 "Those who are ashamed of me and of my words, of them the Son of Man will be ashamed when he comes in his glory and the glory of the Father and of the holy angels." |

In today's age of political correctness, it's easy to avoid talking about Jesus and his teachings, even for those who really have something to share. And, just as we express our shame for criminal or incompetent relatives by avoiding any mention of them, we express our shame for Jesus by avoiding any mention of him.

Friend at midnight

> Luke 11: 5 And he said to them, "Suppose one of you has a friend, and you go to him at midnight and say to him, 'Friend, lend me three loaves of bread;
> 6 for a friend of mine has arrived, and I have nothing to set before him.'
> 7 And he answers from within, 'Do not bother me; the door has already been locked, and my children are with me in bed; I cannot get up and give you anything.'
> 8 I tell you, even though he will not get up and give him anything because he is his friend, at least because of his persistence he will get up and give him whatever he needs."

The first thing to notice here is that we are dealing with a friend, not some wealthy stranger that we only approach when we are in dire need. This friend is someone we know well enough to approach persistently even at awkward times.

Our challenge, of course, is to be sure that we are not strangers to the creator god. If we only turn to him in times of need we have no right to expect a friend's answers to our petitions.

Laborers in vineyard

> Matt. 20: 1 "For the kingdom of heaven is like a landowner who went out early in the morning to hire laborers for his vineyard.
> 2 After agreeing with the laborers for the usual daily wage, he sent them into his vineyard.
> 3 When he went out about nine o'clock, he saw others standing idle in the marketplace;
> 4 and he said to them, 'You also go into the vineyard, and I will pay you whatever is right'. So they went.
> 5 When he went out again about noon and about three o'clock, he did the same.
> 6 And about five o'clock he went out and found others standing

> around; and he said to them, 'Why are you standing here idle all day?'
> 7 They said to him, 'Because no one has hired us.' He said to them, 'You also go into the vineyard.'
> 8 When evening came, the owner of the vineyard said to his manager, 'Call the laborers and give them their pay, beginning with the last and then going to the first.'
> 9 When those hired about five o'clock came, each of them received the usual daily wage.
> 10 Now when the first came, they thought they would receive more; but each of them also received the usual daily wage.
> 11 And when they received it, they grumbled against the landowner,
> 12 saying, 'These last worked only one hour, and you have made them equal to us who have borne the burden of the day and the scorching heat.'
> 13 But he replied to one of them, 'Friend, I am doing you no wrong; did you not agree with me for the usual daily wage?
> 14 Take what belongs to you and go; I choose to give to this last the same as I give to you.
> 15 Am I not allowed to do what I choose with what belongs to me? Or are you envious because I am generous?'
> 16 So the last will be first, and the first will be last."

This lesson, unwelcome as it may be in the church, tells us that even those who don't choose to follow Christ until they become old will enjoy the treasures of heaven as much as those who choose while they are still young. The latter, of course, will spend more years doing God's work free of the uncertainty about their eternal life.

We don't know whether Constantine knew the meaning of this parable, but it's reported that he did not convert to Christianity until he was on his deathbed. (And even then his baptism may have been involuntary.) It could well be argued that much of his life was spent doing God's work despite his lack of public conversion. It could also be argued that Constantine launched 'the church' on its path to worldliness. In that case, of course, he was serving Mammon rather than the creator god.

Unjust judge

> Like 18: 1 Then Jesus told them a parable about their need to pray always and not to lose heart.
> 2 He said, "In a certain city there was a judge who neither feared God nor had respect for people.
> 3 In that city there was a widow who kept coming to him and saying, 'Grant me justice against my opponent.'
> 4 For a while he refused; but later he said to himself, 'Though I have no fear of God and no respect for anyone,
> 5 yet because this widow keeps bothering me, I will grant her justice, so that she may not wear me out by continually coming.'"
> 6 And the Lord said, "Listen to what the unjust judge says.
> 7 And will not God grant justice to his chosen ones who cry to him day and night? Will he delay long in helping them?
> 8 I tell you, he will quickly grant justice to them. And yet, when the Son of Man comes, will he find faith on earth?"

Jesus encourages believers to ask persistently in faith for those things that are pleasing to God. The teaching goes beyond 'positive thinking' in its emphasis on God's desires.

It seems obvious that many of our prayers are not answered. And it is legitimate to ask whether we are doing something wrong when we pray.

Jesus knew man. And he obviously questioned whether men could put faith in his teachings ahead of their own desires and ahead of Mammon.

In some ways this parable seems to contradict Jesus' teachings about God's awareness of our needs even before we ask.[11]

---

[11] Matt. 6: 8; 6: 28-33 and Luke 12: 27-31.

Two debtors

> Luke 7: 41 "A certain creditor had two debtors; one owed five hundred denarii, and the other fifty.
> 42 When they could not pay, he canceled the debts for both of them. Now which of them will love him more?"
> 43 Simon answered, "I suppose the one for whom he canceled the greater debt." And Jesus said to him, "You have judged rightly."

Here Jesus alerts 'good people' to the likelihood that they will love God less than do repentant sinners. The teaching is not intended to encourage sin. Rather it is intended to encourage 'good people' to acknowledge how much they have sinned and how much God has forgiven them.

Two sons

> Matt. 21: 28 "What do you think? A man had two sons; he went to the first and said, 'Son, go and work in the vineyard today.'
> 29 He answered, 'I will not'; but later he changed his mind and went.
> 30 The father went to the second and said the same; and he answered, 'I go, sir'; but he did not go.
> 31 Which of the two did the will of his father?" They said, "The first." Jesus said to them, "Truly I tell you, the tax collectors and the prostitutes are going into the kingdom of God ahead of you.
> 32 For John came to you in the way of righteousness and you did not believe him, but the tax collectors and the prostitutes believed him; and even after you saw it, you did not change your minds and believe him."

The lesson is obvious: No matter how much we profess our belief in Jesus and our obedience to God, only those who actually obey his instructions will enter his kingdom.

Leavened bread

Matt. 13: 33 He told them another parable: "The kingdom of heaven is like yeast that a woman took and mixed in with three measures of flour until all of it was leavened."	Luke 13: 20 And again he said, "To what should I compare the kingdom of God? 21 It is like yeast that a woman took and mixed in with three measures of flour until all of it was leavened."

Jesus encourages believers with the promise that those who surrender to the kingdom will discover that even a small starting effort, as it is worked into their attitudes and behavior, can raise up and flavor all of their lives over time.

And the creator god can use this same leaven in you to raise up faith in the lives of those you influence.

Wedding banquet

Matt. 22: 1 Once more Jesus spoke to them in parables, saying:
2 "The kingdom of heaven may be compared to a king who gave a wedding banquet for his son.
3 He sent his slaves to call those who had been invited to the wedding banquet, but they would not come.
4 Again he sent other slaves, saying, 'Tell those who have been invited: Look, I have prepared my dinner, my oxen and my fat calves have been slaughtered, and everything is ready; come to the wedding banquet.'
5 But they made light of it and went away, one to his farm, another to his business,
6 while the rest seized his slaves, mistreated them, and killed them.
7 The king was enraged. He sent his troops, destroyed those murderers, and burned their city.
8 Then he said to his slaves, 'The wedding is ready, but those invited were not worthy.
9 Go therefore into the main streets, and invite everyone you find

> to the wedding banquet.'
> 10 Those slaves went out into the streets and gathered all whom they found, both good and bad; so the wedding hall was filled with guests.
> 11 But when the king came in to see the guests, he noticed a man there who was not wearing a wedding robe,
> 12 and he said to him, 'Friend, how did you get in here without a wedding robe?' And he was speechless.
> 13 Then the king said to the attendants, 'Bind him hand and foot, and throw him into the outer darkness, where there will be weeping and gnashing of teeth.'
> 14 For many are called, but few are chosen."

This parable was intended as a condemnation of those Jews who refused to accept Jesus as the messiah for a variety of worldly reasons. The invitation they refused was then extended to sinners, Samaritans and Gentiles.

Many are called to the feast, but it is obedience to God's will that clothes us for the occasion.

The same condemnation extends to self-righteous church members today if they put their own interests or those of 'the church' ahead of Jesus' teachings. Surely it presents a cause for concern for those churches which preach that Jesus wants his followers to be rich.

(See also the parable of Dinner guests: p. 111.)

Love Your Neighbor

Time after time Jesus pictured love as something totally unselfish. To love our friends and family members is not enough. Even sinners and Gentiles eagerly do that. The Christian is called to view all of mankind, attractive and unattractive, individually and collectively, as objects of his love.

Good Samaritan

> Luke 10: 25 Just then a lawyer stood up to test Jesus. "Teacher," he said, "what must I do to inherit eternal life?"
> 26 He said to him, "What is written in the law? What do you read there?"
> 27 He answered, "You shall love the Lord your God with all your heart, and with all your soul, and with all your strength, and with all your mind; and your neighbor as yourself."
> 28 And he said to him, "You have given the right answer; do this, and you will live."
> 29 But wanting to justify himself, he asked Jesus, "And who is my neighbor?"
> 30 Jesus replied, "A man was going down from Jerusalem to Jericho, and fell into the hands of robbers, who stripped him, beat him, and went away, leaving him half dead.
> 31 Now by chance a priest was going down that road; and when he saw him, he passed by on the other side.
> 32 So likewise a Levite, when he came to the place and saw him, passed by on the other side.
> 33 But a Samaritan while traveling came near him; and when he saw him, he was moved with pity.
> 34 He went to him and bandaged his wounds, having poured oil and wine on them. Then he put him on his own animal, brought him to an inn, and took care of him.
> 35 The next day he took out two denarii, gave them to the innkeeper, and said, 'Take care of him; and when I come back, I will repay you whatever more you spend.'
> 36 Which of these three, do you think, was a neighbor to the man who fell into the hands of the robbers?"
> 37 He said, "The one who showed him mercy." Jesus said to him, "Go and do likewise."

As much as we love this story, most of us are more likely to follow the examples of the priest and the Levite. In America we have invested all sorts of government agencies and charitable organizations with responsibility for the downtrodden. Yet we accept only a token responsibility for that ministry for ourselves and for our congregations.

Church expenditures for salaries and buildings and other amenities far surpass expenditures for ministry to the poor, especially if the poor are not affiliated with the congregation. Even the Salvation Army squanders collections on princely houses of worship. Few of us see the poor or mistreated as a personal, or even a congregational, responsibility.

Thousands of church members have journeyed to New Orleans and the Gulf Coast to minister to hurricane victims. Millions of church members have stayed home and ignored the needs of their neighbors in the inner city of every American community.

Paying taxes for welfare programs is not the same as showing mercy, as an individual, for a 'neighbor.' What have you and your fellow church members done?

Great physician

| Matt. 9: 10 And as he sat at dinner in the house, many tax collectors and sinners came and were sitting with him and his disciples.

11 When the Pharisees saw this, they said to his disciples, "Why does your teacher eat with tax collectors and sinners?" | Mark 2: 15 And as he sat at dinner in Levi's house, many tax collectors and sinners were also sitting with Jesus and his disciples-- for there were many who followed him. 16 When the scribes of the Pharisees saw that he was eating with sinners and tax collectors, they said to his disciples, "Why does he eat | Luke 5: 29 Then Levi gave a great banquet for him in his house; and there was a large crowd of tax collectors and others sitting at the table with them.

30 The Pharisees and their scribes were complaining to his disciples, saying, "Why do you eat and drink with tax collectors and sinners?" |

	with tax collectors and sinners?"	
12 But when he heard this, he said, "Those who are well have no need of a physician, but those who are sick.	17 When Jesus heard this, he said to them, "Those who are well have no need of a physician, but those who are sick; I have come to call not the righteous but sinners."	31 Jesus answered, "Those who are well have no need of a physician, but those who are sick; 32 I have come to call not the righteous but sinners to repentance."

In too many churches today financial resources are squandered on comforting 'the saved' rather than on reaching out to the lost. Too many church members are satisfied with their congregational *status quo* rather than hungry for the souls of sinners.

And our churches are filled with too many 'good people' who fail to recognize their spiritual sickness.

Unmerciful servant

Matt. 18: 21 Then Peter came and said to him, "Lord, if another member of the church sins against me, how often should I forgive? As many as seven times?"
22 Jesus said to him, "Not seven times, but, I tell you, seventy-seven times.
23 For this reason the kingdom of heaven may be compared to a king who wished to settle accounts with his slaves.
24 When he began the reckoning, one who owed him ten thousand talents was brought to him;
25 and, as he could not pay, his lord ordered him to be sold, together with his wife and children and all his possessions, and payment to be made.
26 So the slave fell on his knees before him, saying, 'Have

> patience with me, and I will pay you everything.'
> 27 And out of pity for him, the lord of that slave released him and forgave him the debt.
> 28 But that same slave, as he went out, came upon one of his fellow slaves who owed him a hundred denarii; and seizing him by the throat, he said, 'Pay what you owe.'
> 29 Then his fellow slave fell down and pleaded with him, 'Have patience with me, and I will pay you.'
> 30 But he refused; then he went and threw him into prison until he would pay the debt.
> 31 When his fellow slaves saw what had happened, they were greatly distressed, and they went and reported to their lord all that had taken place.
> 32 Then his lord summoned him and said to him, 'You wicked slave! I forgave you all that debt because you pleaded with me.
> 33 Should you not have had mercy on your fellow slave, as I had mercy on you?'
> 34 And in anger his lord handed him over to be tortured until he would pay his entire debt.
> 35 So my heavenly Father will also do to every one of you, if you do not forgive your brother or sister from your heart."

Here is another of Jesus' impossible and unrealistic expectations. The very idea that we should forgive someone who offends us or who legally and morally owes us something, especially money, seems more than even a 'Christian' should be asked to do. To do so repeatedly is the height of foolishness. This is obviously more foolish if we believe that the money is really ours rather than something we administer as stewards for God.

Witness/Be fruitful

Perhaps nothing was so important to Jesus as was spreading the truth of his teachings. And his commandments do not present evangelizing as the responsibility of only a select few. Instead he seemed to expect all who believed him and practiced his teachings to share them with all who would listen.

For hundreds of years, however, church members, with the tacit collusion of their leaders, have abdicated this responsibility. They have assigned it to their preachers/pastors/priests. In the process, evangelism has become much more complicated and difficult than it needs to be. It has become less meaningful as well.

Too often, church members are allowed to believe they have witnessed to Jesus when they have really witnessed to the charisma of their particular church or its leaders. Too often we invite people to come to our church to 'hear the word' rather than sharing the word ourselves.

Grain of wheat

John 12: 24 "Very truly, I tell you, unless a grain of wheat falls into the earth and dies, it remains just a single grain; but if it dies, it bears much fruit."

Jesus used this parable to encourage witnesses. He encourages us to take heart even though our words seem to die as they fall on deaf ears. Surely only a small percentage of those who heard Jesus believed him and learned from him. Even fewer followed him to the cross.

The teaching also comforts those who might die for the cause with the promise of much fruitfulness.

Barren fig tree

Luke 13: 6 Then he told this parable: "A man had a fig tree planted in his vineyard; and he came looking for fruit on it and found none.
7 So he said to the gardener, 'See here! For three years I have come looking for fruit on this fig tree, and still I find none. Cut it down! Why should it be wasting the soil?'
8 He replied, 'Sir, let it alone for one more year, until I dig around it and put manure on it.

> 9 If it bears fruit next year, well and good; but if not, you can cut it down.'"

Here, again, Jesus criticizes 'believers' who look good to the eye but bear no fruit. If we continue fruitless we can be sure that we will be cut off from God's kingdom.

Christian light

Matt. 5: 14 "You are the light of the world. A city built on a hill cannot be hid. 15 No one after lighting a lamp puts it under the bushel basket, but on the lampstand, and it gives light to all in the house. 16 In the same way, let your light shine before others, so that they may see your good works and give glory to your Father in heaven."	Mark 4: 21 He said to them, "Is a lamp brought in to be put under the bushel basket, or under the bed, and not on the lampstand? 22 For there is nothing hidden, except to be disclosed; nor is anything secret, except to come to light. 23 Let anyone with ears to hear listen!"	Luke 8: 16 "No one after lighting a lamp hides it under a jar, or puts it under a bed, but puts it on a lampstand, so that those who enter may see the light. 17 For nothing is hidden that will not be disclosed, nor is anything secret that will not become known and come to light. 18 Then pay attention to how you listen; for to those who have, more will be given;

		and from those who do not have, even what they seem to have will be taken away."

Jesus clearly expects those who have experienced the enlightenment of salvation to share it with others. He also promises that those who have faith will receive more. And those who only appear to have faith will have even that appearance taken away.

Growing seed

> Mark 4: 26 He also said, "The kingdom of God is as if someone would scatter seed on the ground,
> 27 and would sleep and rise night and day, and the seed would sprout and grow, he does not know how.
> 28 The earth produces of itself, first the stalk, then the head, then the full grain in the head.
> 29 But when the grain is ripe, at once he goes in with his sickle, because the harvest has come."

Here, Jesus encourages believers to persist in spreading the word even though they may not see an immediate result of their efforts.

Householder

> Matt. 13: 52 And he said to them, "Therefore every scribe who has been trained for the kingdom of heaven is like the master of a household who brings out of his treasure what is new and what is old."

Jesus encourages believers to look beyond the confines of Jewish teachings to share the new concepts he is presenting.

The sower

| Matt. 13: 3 And he told them many things in parables, saying: "Listen! A sower went out to sow. 4 And as he sowed, some seeds fell on the path, and the birds came and ate them up. 5 Other seeds fell on rocky ground, where they did not have much soil, and they sprang up quickly, since they had no depth of soil. 6 But when the sun rose, they were scorched; and since they had no root, they withered away. 7 Other seeds fell among thorns, and the thorns grew up and choked them. 8 Other seeds fell on good soil and brought forth grain, | Mark 4: 3 "Listen! A sower went out to sow. 4 And as he sowed, some seed fell on the path, and the birds came and ate it up. 5 Other seed fell on rocky ground, where it did not have much soil, and it sprang up quickly, since it had no depth of soil. 6 And when the sun rose, it was scorched; and since it had no root, it withered away. 7 Other seed fell among thorns, and the thorns grew up and choked it, and it yielded no grain. 8 Other seed fell into good soil and brought forth grain, | Luke 8: 5 "A sower went out to sow his seed; and as he sowed, some fell on the path and was trampled on, and the birds of the air ate it up. 6 Some fell on the rock; and as it grew up, it withered for lack of moisture. 7 Some fell among thorns, and the thorns grew with it and choked it. 8 Some fell into good soil, and when it grew, it produced |

some a hundredfold, some sixty, some thirty.	growing up and increasing and yielding thirty and sixty and a hundredfold."	a hundredfold."
9 Let anyone with ears listen!"	9 And he said, "Let anyone with ears to hear listen!"	As he said this, he called out, "Let anyone with ears to hear listen!"
10 Then the disciples came and asked him, "Why do you speak to them in parables?"	10 When he was alone, those who were around him along with the twelve asked him about the parables.	9 Then his disciples asked him what this parable meant.
11 He answered, "To you it has been given to know the secrets of the kingdom of heaven, but to them it has not been given. 12 For to those who have, more will be given, and they will have an abundance; but from those who have nothing, even what they have will be taken away.	11 And he said to them, "To you has been given the secret of the kingdom of God,	10 He said, "To you it has been given to know the secrets of the kingdom of God;
13 The reason I speak to them in parables is that 'seeing they do not perceive, and hearing they do not listen, nor do they	but for those outside, everything comes in parables; 12 in order that 'they may indeed look, but not perceive, and may	but to others I speak in parables, so that 'looking they may not perceive, and listening they may not understand.'

understand.'
14 With them indeed is fulfilled the prophecy of Isaiah that says: 'You will indeed listen, but never understand, and you will indeed look, but never perceive.
15 For this people's heart has grown dull, and their ears are hard of hearing, and they have shut their eyes; so that they might not look with their eyes, and listen with their ears, and understand with their heart and turn- - and I would heal them.'
16 But blessed are your eyes, for they see, and your ears, for they hear.
17 Truly I tell you, many prophets and righteous people longed to see what you see, but did not see it, and to hear what you hear, but did not hear it.

indeed listen, but not understand; so that they may not turn again and be forgiven.'"
13 And he said to them, "Do you not understand this parable? Then how will you understand all the parables?

18 Hear then the parable of the sower. 19 When anyone hears the word of the kingdom and does not understand it, the evil one comes and snatches away what is sown in the heart; this is what was sown on the path. 20 As for what was sown on rocky ground, this is the one who hears the word and immediately receives it with joy; 21 yet such a person has no root, but endures only for a while, and when trouble or persecution arises on account of the word, that person immediately falls away. 22 As for what was sown among thorns, this is the one who hears the word, but	14 The sower sows the word. 15 These are the ones on the path where the word is sown: when they hear, Satan immediately comes and takes away the word that is sown in them. 16 And these are the ones sown on rocky ground: when they hear the word, they immediately receive it with joy. 17 But they have no root, and endure only for a while; then, when trouble or persecution arises on account of the word, immediately they fall away. 18 And others are those sown among the thorns: these are the ones who hear	11 Now the parable is this: The seed is the word of God. 12 The ones on the path are those who have heard; then the devil comes and takes away the word from their hearts, so that they may not believe and be saved. 13 The ones on the rock are those who, when they hear the word, receive it with joy. But these have no root; they believe only for a while and in a time of testing fall away. 14 As for what fell among the thorns, these are the ones who hear; but as they go on their

the cares of the world and the lure of wealth choke the word, and it yields nothing. 23 But as for what was sown on good soil, this is the one who hears the word and understands it, who indeed bears fruit and yields, in one case a hundredfold, in another sixty, and in another thirty."	the word, 19 but the cares of the world, and the lure of wealth, and the desire for other things come in and choke the word, and it yields nothing. 20 And these are the ones sown on the good soil: they hear the word and accept it and bear fruit, thirty and sixty and a hundredfold."	way, they are choked by the cares and riches and pleasures of life, and their fruit does not mature. 15 But as for that in the good soil, these are the ones who, when they hear the word, hold it fast in an honest and good heart, and bear fruit with patient endurance."

    Note that even those people closest to Jesus sometimes failed to understand his parables. And he purposely used parables to confound the masses who heard him. Church members and others today still fail to understand the threats and promises of this parable. Too often they put their faith in membership in the church and its community rather than in Jesus himself.

    In today's church, as in Jesus' world, there is a group who will hear his teachings and ignore or refuse them. These are the people Satan snatches up without any difficulty.

    The second group is those who receive Jesus' teachings with joy and follow him as long as it is fun and popular. But, when they begin to feel uncomfortable, or unpopular or criticized (even to the point of persecution), they lose faith in the good news and turn away. History tells us that many members of the church in Rome denied Jesus when threatened with persecution. A few, sometimes grudgingly, were allowed to rejoin the church when the persecutions stopped.

The third group is those who are so preoccupied with wealth and power and other worldly concerns that they can find no room for Jesus' teachings in their lives.

And the fourth group is composed of those who hear the good news, let it grow within themselves, and then share it with others.

People who worship the church instead of the savior often fail to recognize what kind of soil they represent. And many remain in the church even though they are fruitless.

Vine and branches

> John 15: 1 "I am the true vine, and my Father is the vinegrower.
> 2 He removes every branch in me that bears no fruit. Every branch that bears fruit he prunes to make it bear more fruit.
> 3 You have already been cleansed by the word that I have spoken to you.
> 4 Abide in me as I abide in you. Just as the branch cannot bear fruit by itself unless it abides in the vine, neither can you unless you abide in me.
> 5 I am the vine, you are the branches. Those who abide in me and I in them bear much fruit, because apart from me you can do nothing.
> 6 Whoever does not abide in me is thrown away like a branch and withers; such branches are gathered, thrown into the fire, and burned.
> 7 If you abide in me, and my words abide in you, ask for whatever you wish, and it will be done for you."

Jesus cautions us to remain in constant touch with him in order to assure our fruitfulness. Many churches today preach the dogma of 'once saved, always saved'. Verse two makes it clear that some who are 'saved' will be fruitless and will be pruned away.

Again he cautions that just being part of the branch (saved) is not enough. We must be fruitful. The fruits he mentions most often, of course, are: following his example in doing God's will and in sharing the good news with others.

Verse seven also makes a powerful promise that serves as a gauge of our faith. If our prayers are not being answered, we need to pursue Jesus' teachings more devotedly.

Be Prepared

Millions of church members can get excited about 'the end times.' Dozens of books and magazines have sold millions of copies of stories playing on the 'signs' of Jesus' return.

His parables dealt with what we should be doing while we await his return. Indeed, when he returns, or even when we see the signs, it will be too late to make up for lost ground.

> Luke 14: 28 "For which of you, intending to build a tower, does not first sit down and estimate the cost, to see whether he has enough to complete it?
> 29 Otherwise, when he has laid a foundation and is not able to finish, all who see it will begin to ridicule him,
> 30 saying, 'This fellow began to build and was not able to finish.'
> 31 Or what king, going out to wage war against another king, will not sit down first and consider whether he is able with ten thousand to oppose the one who comes against him with twenty thousand?
> 32 If he cannot, then, while the other is still far away, he sends a delegation and asks for the terms of peace."

It's important to recognize that being a Christian carries a price. Many of those who followed Jesus ceased following him when his demands became too uncomfortable. Salvation through grace may be free, but living out our new lives as Christians can be costly. Thousands who heard Christ, even some disciples,[12] were not willing to pay the price. Millions of church members over the centuries have been equally unwilling.

It behooves each of us to consider the cost of following Jesus (including going to the cross) before we convince ourselves that we are being faithful.

Alert servants

Mark 13: 33 "Beware, keep alert; for you do not know when the time will come.
34 It is like a man going on a journey, when he leaves home and puts his slaves in charge, each with his work, and commands the doorkeeper to be on the watch.
35 Therefore, keep awake—for you do not know when the master of the house will come, in the evening, or at midnight, or at cockcrow, or at dawn,
36 or else he may find you asleep when he comes suddenly.
37 And what I say to you I say to all: Keep awake."

Time after time Jesus reminded his followers to be prepared for the coming of his kingdom. We must keep in mind that our opportunity to choose Jesus expires when this body dies So we should not hesitate to choose just because we don't see any signs of the end of the earth. And those who have chosen Jesus need to be continually at work doing those things God has called us to do.

Ten virgins

Matt. 25: 1 "Then the kingdom of heaven will be like this. Ten bridesmaids took their lamps and went to meet the bridegroom.

---

[12] John 6: 64-66.

> 2 Five of them were foolish, and five were wise.
> 3 When the foolish took their lamps, they took no oil with them;
> 4 but the wise took flasks of oil with their lamps.
> 5 As the bridegroom was delayed, all of them became drowsy and slept.
> 6 But at midnight there was a shout, 'Look! Here is the bridegroom! Come out to meet him.'
> 7 Then all those bridesmaids got up and trimmed their lamps.
> 8 The foolish said to the wise, 'Give us some of your oil, for our lamps are going out.'
> 9 But the wise replied, 'No! there will not be enough for you and for us; you had better go to the dealers and buy some for yourselves.'
> 10 And while they went to buy it, the bridegroom came, and those who were ready went with him into the wedding banquet; and the door was shut.
> 11 Later the other bridesmaids came also, saying, 'Lord, lord, open to us.'
> 12 But he replied, 'Truly I tell you, I do not know you.'
> 13 Keep awake therefore, for you know neither the day nor the hour."

On first consideration, this seems to be in contradiction to Jesus' teaching that we should do unto others as we would have them do unto us. However, it might also be an extension of his teaching not to cast our pearls before swine since the foolish virgins had neglected to make the common sense preparations while it was still light.

Don't lose sight of the principle that we should be doing God's will every moment as if he were at the door right now.

Unclean spirit

Matt. 12: 43 "When the unclean spirit has gone out of a person, it wanders through waterless regions looking for a resting	Luke 11: 24 "When the unclean spirit has gone out of a person, it wanders through waterless regions looking for a resting

place, but it finds none. 44 Then it says, 'I will return to my house from which I came'. When it comes, it finds it empty, swept, and put in order. 45 Then it goes and brings along seven other spirits more evil than itself, and they enter and live there; and the last state of that person is worse than the first. So will it be also with this evil generation."	place, but not finding any, it says, 'I will return to my house from which I came.' 25 When it comes, it finds it swept and put in order. 26 Then it goes and brings seven other spirits more evil than itself, and they enter and live there; and the last state of that person is worse than the first."

Many churches teach that once a person is saved they are always saved. This parable and other teachings seem to contradict the 'always saved' idea. Unless we are diligent in building and maintaining our relationship with God, we are vulnerable to so-called 'backsliding' into a condition worse than what we knew before our salvation.

Watching slaves

Luke 12: 35 "Be dressed for action and have your lamps lit;
36 be like those who are waiting for their master to return from the wedding banquet, so that they may open the door for him as soon as he comes and knocks.
37 Blessed are those slaves whom the master finds alert when he comes; truly I tell you, he will fasten his belt and have them sit down to eat, and he will come and serve them.
38 If he comes during the middle of the night, or near dawn, and finds them so, blessed are those slaves.
39 "But know this: if the owner of the house had known at what hour the thief was coming, he would not have let his house be broken into.
40 You also must be ready, for the Son of Man is coming at an unexpected hour."

Once again, Jesus warns his followers to be prepared. It's important to consider that your opportunity to receive salvation expires the moment your mortal body dies.

Wise slave

Matt. 24: 45 "Who then is the faithful and wise slave, whom his master has put in charge of his household, to give the other slaves their allowance of food at the proper time? 46 Blessed is that slave whom his master will find at work when he arrives. 47 Truly I tell you, he will put that one in charge of all his possessions.	Luke 12: 42 And the Lord said, "Who then is the faithful and prudent manager whom his master will put in charge of his slaves, to give them their allowance of food at the proper time? 43 Blessed is that slave whom his master will find at work when he arrives. 44 Truly I tell you, he will put that one in charge of all his possessions.
48 But if that wicked slave says to himself, 'My master is delayed,' 49 and he begins to beat his fellow slaves, and eats and drinks with drunkards, 50 the master of that slave will come on a day when he does not expect him and at an hour that he does not know. 51 He will cut him in pieces and put him with the hypocrites, where there will be weeping and gnashing of teeth."	45 But if that slave says to himself, 'My master is delayed in coming,' and if he begins to beat the other slaves, men and women, and to eat and drink and get drunk, 46 the master of that slave will come on a day when he does not expect him and at an hour that he does not know, and will cut him in pieces, and put him with the unfaithful. 47 That slave who knew what his master wanted, but did not

	prepare himself or do what was wanted, will receive a severe beating. 48 But the one who did not know and did what deserved a beating will receive a light beating. From everyone to whom much has been given, much will be required; and from the one to whom much has been entrusted, even more will be demanded."

Jesus cautions his followers to practice good stewardship of all that has been entrusted to them. To abuse or neglect our neighbors or to waste the blessings entrusted to us is a sure road to condemnation.

He also emphasizes that men and women who know God's will and neglect or refuse to do it are in greater danger than people who never knew God's will.

Children in the marketplace

Matt. 11: 16 "But to what will I compare this generation? It is like children sitting in the marketplaces and calling to one another, 17 'We played the flute for you, and you did not dance; we wailed, and you did not mourn.' 18 For John came neither eating nor drinking, and they say, 'He has a demon';	Luke 7: 31 "To what then will I compare the people of this generation, and what are they like? 32 They are like children sitting in the marketplace and calling to one another, 'We played the flute for you, and you did not dance; we wailed, and you did not weep.' 33 For John the Baptist has come eating no bread and drinking no wine, and you say,

19 the Son of Man came eating and drinking, and they say, 'Look, a glutton and a drunkard, a friend of tax collectors and sinners!' Yet wisdom is vindicated by her deeds."	'He has a demon'; 34 the Son of Man has come eating and drinking, and you say, 'Look, a glutton and a drunkard, a friend of tax collectors and sinners!' 35 Nevertheless, wisdom is vindicated by all her children."

Jesus does not call us out of the world to the comfort and security of an exclusive church. Instead he calls us to go into the, sometimes uncomfortable, world to minister to sinners and those in need. And he promises our wisdom and faithfulness will be defined and judged on the basis of our fruitfulness.

Signs of the end

Matt. 24: 26 "So, if they say to you, 'Look! He is in the wilderness,' do not go out. If they say, 'Look! He is in the inner rooms,' do not believe it. 27 For as the lightning comes from the east and flashes as far as the west, so will be the coming of the Son of Man. 28 Wherever the corpse is, there the vultures will gather. 29 Immediately after the suffering	Mark 13: 21 "And if anyone says to you at that time, 'Look! Here is the Messiah!' or 'Look! There he is!'--do not believe it. 22 False messiahs and false prophets will appear and produce signs and omens, to lead astray, if possible, the elect. 23 But be alert; I have already told you everything. 24 But in those days, after that suffering, the sun	Luke 21: 20 "When you see Jerusalem surrounded by armies, then know that its desolation has come near. 21 Then those in Judea must flee to the mountains, and those inside the city must leave it, and those out in the country must not enter it; 22 for these are days of vengeance, as a fulfillment of all that is written. 23 Woe to those who are pregnant

of those days the sun will be darkened, and the moon will not give its light; the stars will fall from heaven, and the powers of heaven will be shaken.	will be darkened, and the moon will not give its light, 25 and the stars will be falling from heaven, and the powers in the heavens will be shaken.	and to those who are nursing infants in those days! For there will be great distress on the earth and wrath against this people; 24 they will fall by the edge of the sword and be taken away as captives among all nations; and Jerusalem will be trampled on by the Gentiles, until the times of the Gentiles are fulfilled. 25 There will be signs in the sun, the moon, and the stars, and on the earth distress among nations confused by the roaring of the sea and the waves. 26 People will faint from fear and foreboding of what is coming upon the world, for the powers of the heavens will be shaken.
30 Then the sign of the Son of Man will appear in heaven,	26 Then they will see 'the Son of Man coming in clouds'	27 Then they will see 'the Son of Man coming in a cloud'

and then all the tribes of the earth will mourn, and they will see 'the Son of Man coming on the clouds of heaven' with power and great glory. 31 And he will send out his angels with a loud trumpet call, and they will gather his elect from the four winds, from one end of heaven to the other.	with great power and glory. 27 Then he will send out the angels, and gather his elect from the four winds, from the ends of the earth to the ends of heaven.	with power and great glory. 28 Now when these things begin to take place, stand up and raise your heads, because your redemption is drawing near."
32 From the fig tree learn its lesson: as soon as its branch becomes tender and puts forth its leaves, you know that summer is near.	28 From the fig tree learn its lesson: as soon as its branch becomes tender and puts forth its leaves, you know that summer is near.	29 Then he told them a parable: "Look at the fig tree and all the trees; 30 as soon as they sprout leaves you can see for yourselves and know that summer is already near.
33 So also, when you see all these things, you know that he is near, at the very gates.	29 So also, when you see these things taking place, you know that he is near, at the very gates.	31 So also, when you see these things taking place, you know that the kingdom of God is near.
34 Truly I tell you, this generation will not pass away until all these things	30 Truly I tell you, this generation will not pass away until all these things	32 Truly I tell you, this generation will not pass away until all things have

have taken place. 35 Heaven and earth will pass away, but my words will not pass away."	have taken place. 31 Heaven and earth will pass away, but my words will not pass away. 32 But about that day or hour no one knows, neither the angels in heaven, nor the Son, but only the Father."	taken place. 33 Heaven and earth will pass away, but my words will not pass away."

An amazing prophecy! And history reports that many prophets have announced the end of the world as imminent.

Perhaps the significant lesson to be learned here is that, no matter when Jesus returns, your opportunity to choose eternal relationship with the creator god expires when you die.

(See also the parable of the Rich man and Lazarus: p. 109.)

Treasures in Heaven

Time after time Jesus told his audiences that the kingdom he promised was at odds with earthly treasures. He clearly portrayed Mammon, the god of possessions, as the enemy of the creator God. He saw Mammon as an enemy in competition for men's souls. And Jesus was determined that men should not put worldly treasures ahead of dependence on God.

But 'the church,' since the days of Constantine, has focused much of its energy and time on accumulating worldly treasures and on building empires.

Matt. 16: 21 From that time on, Jesus began to show his	Mark 8: 31 Then he began to teach them that the Son of Man

disciples that he must go to Jerusalem and undergo great suffering at the hands of the elders and chief priests and scribes, and be killed, and on the third day be raised. 22 And Peter took him aside and began to rebuke him, saying, "God forbid it, Lord! This must never happen to you. 23 But he turned and said to Peter, "Get behind me, Satan! You are a stumbling block to me; for you are setting your mind not on divine things but on human things."	must undergo great suffering, and be rejected by the elders, the chief priests, and the scribes, and be killed, and after three days rise again. 32 He said all this quite openly. And Peter took him aside and began to rebuke him. 33 But turning and looking at his disciples, he rebuked Peter and said, "Get behind me, Satan! For you are setting your mind not on divine things but on human things."

Today the church is on the brink of a chasm greater than the Reformation. Some churches are bent on selling a reinvented god to their members with the promise of treasures in this world and eternal life. These churches seek a god they can touch just as the Jews did in the wilderness when they prevailed on Aaron to make them a golden calf.

The church of our fathers still pays lip-service to the suffering Jesus and dependence on God (though the church is sometimes full of greed and pride and self-centeredness).

Surely two such different interpretations of God cannot both be legitimate. This means that millions of church members, in one camp or the other, or both, are destined for Hell.

Matt. 16: 25 "For those who want to save their life will lose it, and those who lose their life for my sake will	Mark 8: 35 "For those who want to save their life will lose it, and those who lose their life for my sake, and for	

find it. 26 For what will it profit them if they gain the whole world but forfeit their life? Or what will they give in return for their life?"	the sake of the gospel, will save it. 36 For what will it profit them to gain the whole world and forfeit their life? 37 Indeed, what can they give in return for their life?"	Luke 9: 25 "What does it profit them if they gain the whole world, but lose or forfeit themselves?"

This teaching only has meaning for people who believe in eternal life. Any church member who does not covet eternal life will surely covet all the 'good' and comfortable things that the worldly wealth of the 'Prosperity Gospel' promises.

But many church members, even those who seek eternal life, have never wrestled with the question of what it means for them to lose their lives for Jesus' sake.

Hidden treasure

Matt. 13: 44 "The kingdom of heaven is like treasure hidden in a field, which someone found and hid; then in his joy he goes and sells all that he has and buys that field."

Here is an unwelcome confirmation that the kingdom of heaven is worth sacrificing all our worldly possessions and ambitions for. Obviously, Jesus is not talking about land. But he is talking about the discipline and sacrifice required to gain the treasure of eternal life. Certainly this kind of sacrifice is almost unheard of in modern churches (even the Roman Catholic orders) either for individuals or for the denominations as a whole.

Imagine how this could be true for you. Then work on your understanding and your compliance with God's will.

Pearl of great price

> Matt. 13: 45 "Again, the kingdom of heaven is like a merchant in search of fine pearls;
> 46 on finding one pearl of great value, he went and sold all that he had and bought it."

Few of Jesus' demands are more uncomfortable for church members than this idea that we should sacrifice all our worldly possessions (or even ten percent of our income) in order to gain entry to heaven. The point is not how much we give. Certainly God does not need our money. And even the widow's mite[13] was sufficient for her offering. The point is that: however much we give, it should be enough to demonstrate our reliance on God for our daily needs.

Rich man and Lazarus

> Luke 16: 19 "There was a rich man who was dressed in purple and fine linen and who feasted sumptuously every day.
> 20 And at his gate lay a poor man named Lazarus, covered with sores,
> 21 who longed to satisfy his hunger with what fell from the rich man's table; even the dogs would come and lick his sores.
> 22 The poor man died and was carried away by the angels to be with Abraham. The rich man also died and was buried.
> 23 In Hades, where he was being tormented, he looked up and saw Abraham far away with Lazarus by his side.
> 24 He called out, 'Father Abraham, have mercy on me, and send Lazarus to dip the tip of his finger in water and cool my tongue; for I am in agony in these flames.'
> 25 But Abraham said, 'Child, remember that during your lifetime you received your good things, and Lazarus in like manner evil things; but now he is comforted here, and you are in agony.

---

[13] Mark 12: 42-43.

> 26 Besides all this, between you and us a great chasm has been fixed, so that those who might want to pass from here to you cannot do so, and no one can cross from there to us.'
> 27 He said, 'Then, father, I beg you to send him to my father's house--
> 28 for I have five brothers--that he may warn them, so that they will not also come into this place of torment.'
> 29 Abraham replied, 'They have Moses and the prophets; they should listen to them.'
> 30 He said, 'No, father Abraham; but if someone goes to them from the dead, they will repent.'
> 31 He said to him, 'If they do not listen to Moses and the prophets, neither will they be convinced even if someone rises from the dead.'"

Clearly, Jesus told his followers that some people would never learn from the prophets or even from him. He promised that Hell awaits those who put worldly possessions ahead of the creator God and their neighbors.

Rich fool

> Luke 12: 16 Then he told them a parable: "The land of a rich man produced abundantly.
> 17 And he thought to himself, 'What should I do, for I have no place to store my crops?'
> 18 Then he said, 'I will do this: I will pull down my barns and build larger ones, and there I will store all my grain and my goods.
> 19 And I will say to my soul, 'Soul, you have ample goods laid up for many years; relax, eat, drink, be merry.'
> 20 But God said to him, 'You fool! This very night your life is being demanded of you. And the things you have prepared, whose will they be?'
> 21 So it is with those who store up treasures for themselves but are not rich toward God."

Jesus reminds us that we have no idea when we might die. And it is vitally important for us to be in good standing with God at every moment. Jesus promises that earthly treasures cannot prolong our lives or assure our salvation.

Righteous vs. Sinners

The essence of sin is to put our own desires ahead of God's desires. Adam and Eve were the first people to commit this sin and all men have been tempted by it. It is at the heart of the first commandment.

Jesus cautioned repeatedly against expecting conventional righteousness to gain your salvation. His world was full of people who were nice to their friends: people who gave to those who could return the gifts: people who gave to causes that would benefit their interests. Jesus stressed that these people would receive their rewards in this life but not in eternal life. Surely, many who heard this teaching could not understand or accept it and the same is true of many today.

Dinner guests

Luke 14: 15 One of the dinner guests, on hearing this, said to him, "Blessed is anyone who will eat bread in the kingdom of God!"
16 Then Jesus said to him, "Someone gave a great dinner and invited many.
17 At the time for the dinner he sent his slave to say to those who had been invited, 'Come; for everything is ready now.'
18 But they all alike began to make excuses. The first said to him, 'I have bought a piece of land, and I must go out and see it; please accept my regrets.'
19 Another said, 'I have bought five yoke of oxen, and I am going to try them out; please accept my regrets.'
20 Another said, 'I have just been married, and therefore I cannot

> come.'
> 21 So the slave returned and reported this to his master. Then the owner of the house became angry and said to his slave, 'Go out at once into the streets and lanes of the town and bring in the poor, the crippled, the blind, and the lame.'
> 22 And the slave said, 'Sir, what you ordered has been done, and there is still room."
> 23 Then the master said to the slave, 'Go out into the roads and lanes, and compel people to come in, so that my house may be filled.
> 24 For I tell you, none of those who were invited will taste my dinner.'"

The desire for worldly possessions and the apparent independence that they promise is one of the most common expressions of sin. Jesus promised that the poor, sick and powerless would fare better in heaven than those who put riches and their personal desires ahead of pleasing God.

(See also the parable of the Wedding banquet: p. 82.)

Feast invitations

> Luke 14: 12 He said also to the one who had invited him, "When you give a luncheon or a dinner, do not invite your friends or your brothers or your relatives or rich neighbors, in case they may invite you in return, and you would be repaid.
> 13 But when you give a banquet, invite the poor, the crippled, the lame, and the blind.
> 14 And you will be blessed, because they cannot repay you, for you will be repaid at the resurrection of the righteous."

Few of Jesus' teachings are more neglected than this one. The Salvation Army seems to hear it, but mostly in an institutional mode. It's hard to imagine a pastor/preacher/priest (especially in a city of any size) encouraging his congregation to actually practice this kind of generosity. Even during the Great Depression the homeless vagrants were expected to work for the hand-outs that many rural families gave them. Most urban church members today would be fearful of inviting the poor and homeless into their homes. Instead, we give occasional and, sometimes, grudging support to government programs and non-profit organizations that we expect to 'look after' the poor and keep them off the streets.

I think it's interesting (and troubling) that thousands of church members will not contribute to The American Red Cross or The United Way or other charities because they perceive that those organizations spend too much on overhead. Many of the same people will contribute generously to churches that spend **all** of their income on salaries, mortgages, creature comforts and other overhead. Few go into their communities to personally minister to the needy.

Jesus' Role

Jesus taught about his role with his words and with his examples. Typically, church members, and others today, pick and choose what we will believe. We sometimes invent and embellish our beliefs to give them precedence over the gospel witness.

Jesus' role was to show mankind the nature of God and to reveal God's plans and promises for mankind (both sinners and those who would believe Jesus). He came to Earth as a messenger from the creator God. He presented himself as a sacrifice for the sins of those who would follow him. And he served as an example men could follow, if they would, **to experience the creator god**. He told his followers that those who had seen what he was like had seen what the father was like.[14]

On several occasions Jesus likened himself to bread or the 'bread of life,' the implication being that he could nourish his followers each day and for eternity.

---

[14] John 14: 9.

Bread of life

> John 6: 31 "Our ancestors ate the manna in the wilderness; as it is written, 'He gave them bread from heaven to eat.'"
> 32 Then Jesus said to them, "Very truly, I tell you, it was not Moses who gave you the bread from heaven, but it is my Father who gives you the true bread from heaven.
> 33 For the bread of God is that which comes down from heaven and gives life to the world."
> 34 They said to him, "Sir, give us this bread always."
> 35 Jesus said to them, "I am the bread of life. Whoever comes to me will never be hungry, and whoever believes in me will never be thirsty.
> 36 But I said to you that you have seen me and yet do not believe.
> 37 Everything that the Father gives me will come to me, and anyone who comes to me I will never drive away;
> 38 for I have come down from heaven, not to do my own will, but the will of him who sent me."

In this passage Jesus does not promise to sustain life as the manna in the wilderness sustained the exiles. Rather, he promises to 'give' life with the implication that that life will last forever. He then pronounces that he is this 'true' bread of God which provides life everlasting. But Jesus explains that there are conditions: men must accept him as the 'bread of life' and they must do God's will just as he does God's will. He makes 'believing in' him much more demanding than a simple profession of faith or recognition of his role. Even many of those who saw him and heard him, even touched him, did not believe enough to follow him.

Verse 37 is sometimes quoted to support the idea that anyone who is 'saved' will always be saved. That is not what Jesus says. Here, and in other places, Jesus leaves the door open for followers to desert him for other temptations just as Judas reputedly did. Indeed, many who followed him for a while dropped away when his teachings became too demanding.[15] And doing God's will is paramount.

Divided kingdom

		Luke 11: 14 Now he was casting out a demon that was mute; when the demon had gone out, the one who had been mute spoke, and the crowds were amazed.
Matt. 12: 24 But when the Pharisees heard it, they said, "It is only by Beelzebul, the ruler of the demons, that this fellow casts out the demons."	Mark 3: 22 And the scribes who came down from Jerusalem said, "He has Beelzebul, and by the ruler of the demons he casts out demons."	15 But some of them said, "He casts out demons by Beelzebul, the ruler of the demons." 16 Others, to test him, kept demanding from him a sign from heaven.
25 He knew what they were thinking and said to them, "Every kingdom divided against itself is laid waste, and no city or house divided against itself will	23 And he called them to him, and spoke to them in parables, "How can Satan cast out Satan? 24 If a kingdom is divided against itself, that kingdom	17 But he knew what they were thinking and said to them, "Every kingdom divided against itself becomes a desert, and house falls on house.

---

[15] John 6: 64-66.

stand. 26 If Satan casts out Satan, he is divided against himself; how then will his kingdom stand?	cannot stand. 25 And if a house is divided against itself, that house will not be able to stand. 26 And if Satan has risen up against himself and is divided, he cannot stand, but his end has come.	18 If Satan also is divided against himself, how will his kingdom stand?
27 If I cast out demons by Beelzebul, by whom do your own exorcists cast them out? Therefore they will be your judges. 28 But if it is by the Spirit of God that I cast out demons, then the kingdom of God has come to you.		--for you say that I cast out the demons by Beelzebul. 19 Now if I cast out the demons by Beelzebul, by whom do your exorcists cast them out? Therefore they will be your judges. 20 But if it is by the finger of God that I cast out the demons, then the kingdom of God has come to you.
29 Or how can one enter a strong man's house and plunder his property, without first tying up the strong man? Then indeed the house can be plundered.	27 But no one can enter a strong man's house and plunder his property without first tying up the strong man; then indeed the house can be plundered."	21 When a strong man, fully armed, guards his castle, his property is safe. 22 But when one stronger than he attacks him and overpowers him, he takes away his

		armor in which he trusted and divides his plunder.
30 Whoever is not with me is against me, and whoever does not gather with me scatters."		23 Whoever is not with me is against me, and whoever does not gather with me scatters."

Here Jesus contrasts himself with Satan and explains that he heals by the spirit of God. He reveals that he has bound Beelzebul, at least temporarily, and is taking the sick and afflicted and sinners from that devil's house. And he goes on to reveal that he has come to gather men to God. He adds the warning that those who don't help him gather are indeed scattering in opposition to God.

Sign of Jonah

Matt. 12: 38 Then some of the scribes and Pharisees said to him, "Teacher, we wish to see a sign from you."	
39 But he answered them, "An evil and adulterous generation asks for a sign, but no sign will be given to it except the sign of the prophet Jonah. 40 For just as Jonah was three days and three nights in the belly of the sea monster, so for three days and three nights the Son of Man will be in the heart of the earth.	Luke 11: 29 When the crowds were increasing, he began to say, "This generation is an evil generation; it asks for a sign, but no sign will be given to it except the sign of Jonah.
41 The people of Nineveh will rise up at the judgment with	Luke 11: 32 "The people of Nineveh will rise up at the

this generation and condemn it, because they repented at the proclamation of Jonah, and see, something greater than Jonah is here!	judgment with this generation and condemn it, because they repented at the proclamation of Jonah, and see, something greater than Jonah is here!"
	Luke 11: 30 "For just as Jonah became a sign to the people of Nineveh, so the Son of Man will be to this generation.
42 The queen of the South will rise up at the judgment with this generation and condemn it, because she came from the ends of the earth to listen to the wisdom of Solomon, and see, something greater than Solomon is here!"	31 The queen of the South will rise at the judgment with the people of this generation and condemn them, because she came from the ends of the earth to listen to the wisdom of Solomon, and see, something greater than Solomon is here!"

It's hard to imagine what kind of sign the Jewish leaders wanted to see. They had already seen miracles of healing. They had probably seen or heard of Jesus feeding the multitudes. They had heard of the miracles his followers performed. Mostly the leaders wanted to embarrass Jesus and justify themselves. And, surely, they recognized his response as a stinging criticism though they probably didn't understand it.

And people (inside and outside the church) still wait for a sign with little evidence of repentance or understanding.

The Lost

Many churches today are filled with good people, generous and friendly. Too often, however, those good people have no sense of having sinned against the creator and therefore they sense no need for repentance or forgiveness. They see no conflict between their life-styles and Jesus' commandments thus they cut themselves off from the creator god.

Lost coin

> Luke 15: 8 "Or what woman having ten silver coins, if she loses one of them, does not light a lamp, sweep the house, and search carefully until she finds it?
> 9 When she has found it, she calls together her friends and neighbors, saying, 'Rejoice with me, for I have found the coin that I had lost.'
> 10 Just so, I tell you, there is joy in the presence of the angels of God over one sinner who repents."

God searches for those who are lost and rejoices when they are found. But there is no indication that God forces repentance, or a new way of seeing their lives and relationships, on anyone. (Paul's experience on the road to Damascus may be an exception to this observation. But Paul was dedicated to the creator god and his epiphany was more a matter of redirection that total rededication.)

The church often comforts those who cannot recognize that they are lost.

Lost sheep

> Luke 15: 4 "Which one of you, having a hundred sheep and losing one of them, does not leave the ninety-nine in the wilderness and

> go after the one that is lost until he finds it?
> 5 When he has found it, he lays it on his shoulders and rejoices.
> 6 And when he comes home, he calls together his friends and neighbors, saying to them, 'Rejoice with me, for I have found my sheep that was lost.'
> 7 Just so, I tell you, there will be more joy in heaven over one sinner who repents than over ninety-nine righteous persons who need no repentance."

Again, Jesus warns that God is happier with one person who has repented and returned to him than he is with all those self-righteous who do not need him.

We may be tempted to believe that we are among the 99 percent who are righteous, but it is important to base our assurance on our fruitfulness rather than on our treasures.

Many church members don't even bother to share the joys of salvation with other members, much less with the lost.

Prodigal son

> Luke 15: 11 Then Jesus said, "There was a man who had two sons.
> 12 The younger of them said to his father, 'Father, give me the share of the property that will belong to me'. So he divided his property between them.
> 13 A few days later the younger son gathered all he had and traveled to a distant country, and there he squandered his property in dissolute living.
> 14 When he had spent everything, a severe famine took place throughout that country, and he began to be in need.
> 15 So he went and hired himself out to one of the citizens of that country, who sent him to his fields to feed the pigs.
> 16 He would gladly have filled himself with the pods that the pigs were eating; and no one gave him anything.
> 17 But when he came to himself he said, 'How many of my father's hired hands have bread enough and to spare, but here I

am dying of hunger!
18 I will get up and go to my father, and I will say to him, "Father, I have sinned against heaven and before you;
19 I am no longer worthy to be called your son; treat me like one of your hired hands."'
20 So he set off and went to his father. But while he was still far off, his father saw him and was filled with compassion; he ran and put his arms around him and kissed him.
21 Then the son said to him, 'Father, I have sinned against heaven and before you; I am no longer worthy to be called your son.'
22 But the father said to his slaves, 'Quickly, bring out a robe--the best one--and put it on him; put a ring on his finger and sandals on his feet.
23 And get the fatted calf and kill it, and let us eat and celebrate;
24 for this son of mine was dead and is alive again; he was lost and is found!' And they began to celebrate.
25 "Now his elder son was in the field; and when he came and approached the house, he heard music and dancing.
26 He called one of the slaves and asked what was going on.
27 He replied, 'Your brother has come, and your father has killed the fatted calf, because he has got him back safe and sound.'
28 Then he became angry and refused to go in. His father came out and began to plead with him.
29 But he answered his father, 'Listen! For all these years I have been working like a slave for you, and I have never disobeyed your command; yet you have never given me even a young goat so that I might celebrate with my friends.
30 But when this son of yours came back, who has devoured your property with prostitutes, you killed the fatted calf for him!'
31 Then the father said to him, 'Son, you are always with me, and all that is mine is yours.
32 But we had to celebrate and rejoice, because this brother of yours was dead and has come to life; he was lost and has been found.'"

This parable is not intended to encourage sinful or wasteful living. It does tell us a great deal about sinful man, the creator god and righteous men.

The prodigal son epitomizes sinfulness: he frees himself from his father and he spends his time and his wealth on self-centered pleasures. He is also bright enough, when his world begins to fall apart, to look at his life in a new way and return to his father's love.

The father is open-minded enough to let his son take a flyer and make mistakes--even wasteful mistakes. He is also loving enough to watch for the return of his son. And he is forgiving enough to welcome his son and ignore his unfortunate behavior.

Interestingly enough, the self-righteous son comes across as an unforgiving, unloving pouter. He obviously feels sorry for himself and blames his father for not giving him things he apparently never asked for.

The parable does not tell us anything about the prodigal's inheritance since he has already wasted his share. But it does hold out hope for the righteous that they will inherit something, despite their resentful lack of forgiveness.

Sorting Sinners from the Saved

Jesus clearly warned that there would be a time when sinners would suffer because of their sins just as the righteous would be rewarded for their good works.

Net of fish

> Matt. 13: 47 "Again, the kingdom of heaven is like a net that was thrown into the sea and caught fish of every kind;
> 48 when it was full, they drew it ashore, sat down, and put the good into baskets but threw out the bad.

> 49 So it will be at the end of the age. The angels will come out and separate the evil from the righteous
> 50 and throw them into the furnace of fire, where there will be weeping and gnashing of teeth."

This teaching is very broad-brush with only general terms (evil and righteous) used to describe the two types of people God will deal with at the end of the age: those who are faithful and those who aren't.

Sheep and goats

> Matt. 25: 31 "When the Son of Man comes in his glory, and all the angels with him, then he will sit on the throne of his glory.
> 32 All the nations will be gathered before him, and he will separate people one from another as a shepherd separates the sheep from the goats,
> 33 and he will put the sheep at his right hand and the goats at the left.
> 34 Then the king will say to those at his right hand, 'Come, you that are blessed by my Father, inherit the kingdom prepared for you from the foundation of the world;
> 35 for I was hungry and you gave me food, I was thirsty and you gave me something to drink, I was a stranger and you welcomed me,
> 36 I was naked and you gave me clothing, I was sick and you took care of me, I was in prison and you visited me.'
> 37 Then the righteous will answer him, 'Lord, when was it that we saw you hungry and gave you food, or thirsty and gave you something to drink?
> 38 And when was it that we saw you a stranger and welcomed you, or naked and gave you clothing?
> 39 And when was it that we saw you sick or in prison and visited you?'
> 40 And the king will answer them, 'Truly I tell you, just as you did it to one of the least of these who are members of my family, you did it to me.'

> 41 Then he will say to those at his left hand, 'You that are accursed, depart from me into the eternal fire prepared for the devil and his angels;
> 42 for I was hungry and you gave me no food, I was thirsty and you gave me nothing to drink,
> 43 I was a stranger and you did not welcome me, naked and you did not give me clothing, sick and in prison and you did not visit me.'
> 44 Then they also will answer, 'Lord, when was it that we saw you hungry or thirsty or a stranger or naked or sick or in prison, and did not take care of you?'
> 45 Then he will answer them, 'Truly I tell you, just as you did not do it to one of the least of these, you did not do it to me.'
> 46 And these will go away into eternal punishment, but the righteous into eternal life."

Here Jesus describes acts of selfish evil and acts of unselfish righteousness in greater detail. It's worth noting that nothing is said here about faith of any kind as a prerequisite for salvation. It's also worth noting that the acts of charity are performed on a person-to-person basis rather than through the church, the government, or through some charitable organization.

Consider what part of its budget your church contributes for the poor who walk the streets of your town or city. Compare that with the amount spent for the comfort of the congregation.

Then consider the amount you contribute in face-to-face concern for the poor.

God will surely consider these things.

Landowner

Matt. 21: 33 "Listen to another parable. There was a landowner who	Mark 12: 1 Then he began to speak to them in parables. "A man planted a	Luke 20: 9 He began to tell the people this parable: "A man planted a vineyard,

planted a vineyard, put a fence around it, dug a wine press in it, and built a watchtower. Then he leased it to tenants and went to another country.	vineyard, put a fence around it, dug a pit for the wine press, and built a watchtower; then he leased it to tenants and went to another country.	and leased it to tenants, and went to another country for a long time.
34 When the harvest time had come, he sent his slaves to the tenants to collect his produce.	2 When the season came, he sent a slave to the tenants to collect from them his share of the produce of the vineyard.	10 When the season came, he sent a slave to the tenants in order that they might give him his share of the produce of the vineyard; but the tenants beat him and sent him away empty-handed.
35 But the tenants seized his slaves and beat one, killed another, and stoned another.	3 But they seized him, and beat him, and sent him away empty-handed.	
36 Again he sent other slaves, more than the first; and they treated them in the same way.	4 And again he sent another slave to them; this one they beat over the head and insulted.	11 Next he sent another slave; that one also they beat and insulted and sent away empty-handed.
	5 Then he sent another, and that one they killed. And so it was with many others; some they beat, and others they killed.	12 And he sent still a third; this one also they wounded and threw out.
37 Finally he sent his son to them, saying, 'They will respect my son.'	6 He had still one other, a beloved son. Finally he sent him to them, saying,	13 Then the owner of the vineyard said, 'What shall I do? I will send my

38 But when the tenants saw the son, they said to themselves, 'This is the heir; come, let us kill him and get his inheritance."	'They will respect my son.' 7 But those tenants said to one another, 'This is the heir; come, let us kill him, and the inheritance will be ours.'	beloved son; perhaps they will respect him.' 14 But when the tenants saw him, they discussed it among themselves and said, 'This is the heir; let us kill him so that the inheritance may be ours.'
39 So they seized him, threw him out of the vineyard, and killed him.	8 So they seized him, killed him, and threw him out of the vineyard.	15 So they threw him out of the vineyard and killed him.
40 Now when the owner of the vineyard comes, what will he do to those tenants?" 41 They said to him, "He will put those wretches to a miserable death, and lease the vineyard to other tenants who will give him the produce at the harvest time."	9 What then will the owner of the vineyard do? He will come and destroy the tenants and give the vineyard to others.	What then will the owner of the vineyard do to them? 16 He will come and destroy those tenants and give the vineyard to others." When they heard this, they said, "Heaven forbid!"
42 Jesus said to them, "Have you never read in the scriptures: 'The stone that the builders rejected has become the	10 Have you not read this scripture: 'The stone that the builders rejected has become the cornerstone; 11 this was the	17 But he looked at them and said, "What then does this text mean: 'The stone that the builders rejected has become the

cornerstone; this was the Lord's doing, and it is amazing in our eyes'? 43 Therefore I tell you, the kingdom of God will be taken away from you and given to a people that produces the fruits of the kingdom. 44 The one who falls on this stone will be broken to pieces; and it will crush anyone on whom it falls."	Lord's doing, and it is amazing in our eyes'?"	cornerstone'? 18 Everyone who falls on that stone will be broken to pieces; and it will crush anyone on whom it falls."

This is easily read as a condemnation of the Jews who received God's bounty but refused to keep their promises to him, even killing his servants and his son.

It can also be read as a condemnation of the church, throughout history: the church that professes to serve God but ignores his demands for obedience and humility; the church that wages war; the church that ignores or neglects the poor.

Tares in the field

> Matt. 13: 24 He put before them another parable: "The kingdom of heaven may be compared to someone who sowed good seed in his field;
> 25 but while everybody was asleep, an enemy came and sowed weeds among the wheat, and then went away.

> 26 So when the plants came up and bore grain, then the weeds appeared as well.
> 27 And the slaves of the householder came and said to him, 'Master, did you not sow good seed in your field? Where, then, did these weeds come from?'
> 28 He answered, 'An enemy has done this'. The slaves said to him, 'Then do you want us to go and gather them?'
> 29 But he replied, 'No; for in gathering the weeds you would uproot the wheat along with them.
> 30 Let both of them grow together until the harvest; and at harvest time I will tell the reapers, Collect the weeds first and bind them in bundles to be burned, but gather the wheat into my barn.'"

Tares in the field (Cont'd.)

> Matt. 13: 36 Then he left the crowds and went into the house. And his disciples approached him, saying, "Explain to us the parable of the weeds of the field."
> 37 He answered, "The one who sows the good seed is the Son of Man;
> 38 the field is the world, and the good seed are the children of the kingdom; the weeds are the children of the evil one,
> 39 and the enemy who sowed them is the devil; the harvest is the end of the age, and the reapers are angels.
> 40 Just as the weeds are collected and burned up with fire, so will it be at the end of the age.
> 41 The Son of Man will send his angels, and they will collect out of his kingdom all causes of sin and all evildoers,
> 42 and they will throw them into the furnace of fire, where there will be weeping and gnashing of teeth.
> 43 Then the righteous will shine like the sun in the kingdom of their Father. Let anyone with ears listen!"

In explaining the coexistence of wheat and weeds in the field, Jesus reminds his listeners that the creator god has 'an enemy' who seeks to corrupt his crop. He warns that uprooting the weeds would uproot the wheat as well. And the landowner tells his servants to leave the sorting until the judgement at harvest time. The enemy has been at work in the church throughout its history. His seeds of corruption grow empire builders and warring denominations. They grow vanity and greed and intolerance and indifference. And they grow monuments of stone and stained glass that glorify congregations and Mammon.

It's interesting that the disciples needed to have the parable explained. But the explanation leaves us with a bright promise as well as a grave admonition.

Disciplines

While most believers accept the promise that salvation is free (grace), Jesus made it clear that the individual who is saved has demanding obligations. If your salvation doesn't set you apart from the unsaved, why bother?

Humbled guest

> Luke 14: 7 When he noticed how the guests chose the places of honor, he told them a parable.
> 8 "When you are invited by someone to a wedding banquet, do not sit down at the place of honor, in case someone more distinguished than you has been invited by your host;
> 9 and the host who invited both of you may come and say to you, 'Give this person your place,' and then in disgrace you would start to take the lowest place.
> 10 But when you are invited, go and sit down at the lowest place, so that when your host comes, he may say to you, 'Friend, move up higher'; then you will be honored in the presence of all who sit at the table with you.
> 11 For all who exalt themselves will be humbled, and those who humble themselves will be exalted."

Here we have a seemingly straightforward lesson that is easily ignored, especially by those with prestige and power and wealth. Humility is no more popular and practiced today than it was in Jesus' time.

Pharisee and tax collector

> Luke 18: 9 He also told this parable to some who trusted in themselves that they were righteous and regarded others with contempt:
> 10 "Two men went up to the temple to pray, one a Pharisee and the other a tax collector.
> 11 The Pharisee, standing by himself, was praying thus, 'God, I thank you that I am not like other people: thieves, rogues, adulterers, or even like this tax collector.
> 12 I fast twice a week; I give a tenth of all my income.'
> 13 But the tax collector, standing far off, would not even look up to heaven, but was beating his breast and saying, 'God, be merciful to me, a sinner!'
> 14 I tell you, this man went down to his home justified rather than the other; for all who exalt themselves will be humbled, but all who humble themselves will be exalted."

Jesus gives us a simple test to measure our sinfulness: if we look down on anyone we are sinners. This is true no matter how sincerely we might justify our wealth or education or power or prestige or righteousness. Prayer and tithing and study and praise don't correct the situation. Only repentance and reformation can effect a cure.

Servant's duty

> Luke 17: 7 "Who among you would say to your slave who has just come in from plowing or tending sheep in the field, 'Come here at once and take your place at the table'?
> 8 Would you not rather say to him, 'Prepare supper for me, put

> on your apron and serve me while I eat and drink; later you may eat and drink'?
> 9 Do you thank the slave for doing what was commanded?
> 10 So you also, when you have done all that you were ordered to do, say, 'We are worthless slaves; we have done only what we ought to have done!'"

Here Jesus paints a picture of humility that is almost impossible to find anywhere in today's world, especially in the leadership of 'the church'.

Unjust steward

> Luke 16: 1 Then Jesus said to the disciples, "There was a rich man who had a manager, and charges were brought to him that this man was squandering his property.
> 2 So he summoned him and said to him, 'What is this that I hear about you? Give me an accounting of your management, because you cannot be my manager any longer.'
> 3 Then the manager said to himself, 'What will I do, now that my master is taking the position away from me? I am not strong enough to dig, and I am ashamed to beg.
> 4 I have decided what to do so that, when I am dismissed as manager, people may welcome me into their homes.'
> 5 So, summoning his master's debtors one by one, he asked the first, 'How much do you owe my master?'
> 6 He answered, 'A hundred jugs of olive oil'. He said to him, 'Take your bill, sit down quickly, and make it fifty.'
> 7 Then he asked another, 'And how much do you owe?' He replied, 'A hundred containers of wheat'. He said to him, 'Take your bill and make it eighty.'
> 8 And his master commended the dishonest manager because he had acted shrewdly; for the children of this age are more shrewd in dealing with their own generation than are the children of light.
> 9 And I tell you, make friends for yourselves by means of dishonest wealth so that when it is gone, they may welcome you into the eternal homes.

> 10 "Whoever is faithful in a very little is faithful also in much; and whoever is dishonest in a very little is dishonest also in much.
> 11 If then you have not been faithful with the dishonest wealth, who will entrust to you the true riches?
> 12 And if you have not been faithful with what belongs to another, who will give you what is your own?
> 13 No slave can serve two masters; for a slave will either hate the one and love the other, or be devoted to the one and despise the other. You cannot serve God and wealth."

Jesus reminds mankind that we are only stewards of the goods the creator god has entrusted to us. If we mismanage our trusts we cheat God and we cheat ourselves of our true riches. It's a pointed reminder that we cannot be equally devoted to money and to the creator god.

Talents and pounds

	Luke 19: 11 As they were listening to this, he went on to tell a parable, because he was near Jerusalem, and because they supposed that the kingdom of God was to appear immediately.
Matt. 25: 14 "For it is as if a man, going on a journey, summoned his slaves and entrusted his property to them; 15 to one he gave five talents, to another two, to another one, to each according to his ability. Then he went away. 16 The one who had received the five talents went off at once and traded with them, and	12 So he said, "A nobleman went to a distant country to get royal power for himself and then return. 13 He summoned ten of his slaves, and gave them ten pounds, and said to them, 'Do business with these until I come back.' 14 But the citizens of his country hated him and sent a

made five more talents. 17 In the same way, the one who had the two talents made two more talents. 18 But the one who had received the one talent went off and dug a hole in the ground and hid his master's money. 19 After a long time the master of those slaves came and settled accounts with them. 20 Then the one who had received the five talents came forward, bringing five more talents, saying, 'Master, you handed over to me five talents; see, I have made five more talents.' 21 His master said to him, 'Well done, good and trustworthy slave; you have been trustworthy in a few things, I will put you in charge of many things; enter into the joy of your master.' 22 And the one with the two talents also came forward, saying, 'Master, you handed over to me two talents; see, I have made two more talents.' 23 His master said to him, 'Well done, good and trustworthy slave; you have been trustworthy in a few	delegation after him, saying, 'We do not want this man to rule over us.' 15 When he returned, having received royal power, he ordered these slaves, to whom he had given the money, to be summoned so that he might find out what they had gained by trading. 16 The first came forward and said, 'Lord, your pound has made ten more pounds.' 17 He said to him, 'Well done, good slave! Because you have been trustworthy in a very small thing, take charge of ten cities.' 18 Then the second came, saying, 'Lord, your pound has made five pounds.' 19 He said to him, 'And you, rule over five cities.'

things, I will put you in charge of many things; enter into the joy of your master.' 24 Then the one who had received the one talent also came forward, saying, 'Master, I knew that you were a harsh man, reaping where you did not sow, and gathering where you did not scatter seed; 25 so I was afraid, and I went and hid your talent in the ground. Here you have what is yours.' 26 But his master replied, 'You wicked and lazy slave! You knew, did you, that I reap where I did not sow, and gather where I did not scatter? 27 Then you ought to have invested my money with the bankers, and on my return I would have received what was my own with interest. 28 So take the talent from him, and give it to the one with the ten talents. 29 For to all those who have, more will be given, and they will have an abundance; but from those who have nothing, even what they have will be taken away.	20 Then the other came, saying, 'Lord, here is your pound. I wrapped it up in a piece of cloth, 21 for I was afraid of you, because you are a harsh man; you take what you did not deposit, and reap what you did not sow.' 22 He said to him, 'I will judge you by your own words, you wicked slave! You knew, did you, that I was a harsh man, taking what I did not deposit and reaping what I did not sow? 23 Why then did you not put my money into the bank? Then when I returned, I could have collected it with interest.' 24 He said to the bystanders, 'Take the pound from him and give it to the one who has ten pounds.' 25 (And they said to him, 'Lord, he has ten pounds!') 26 'I tell you, to all those who have, more will be given; but from those who have nothing, even what they have will be taken away.

| 30 As for this worthless slave, throw him into the outer darkness, where there will be weeping and gnashing of teeth.'" | 27 But as for these enemies of mine who did not want me to be king over them--bring them here and slaughter them in my presence.'" |

The parable makes abundantly clear the fact that God may love many people enough to give them 'talents' in trust. But two other things are abundantly clear: 1) those of us who are given 'seed money' (in whatever form) and make no effort to grow it for God's benefit will be punished; and 2) those of us who reject God's rulership will die.

It's interesting that nothing is said in Luke about the performance of the other seven servants.

Mustard seed

| Matt. 13: 31 He put before them another parable:

"The kingdom of heaven is like a mustard seed that someone took and sowed in his field; 32 it is the smallest of all the seeds, but when it has grown it is the greatest of shrubs and becomes a tree, so that the birds of the air come and make | Mark 4: 30 He also said, "With what can we compare the kingdom of God, or what parable will we use for it? 31 It is like a mustard seed, which, when sown upon the ground, is the smallest of all the seeds on earth; 32 yet when it is sown it grows up and becomes the greatest of all shrubs, and puts forth large branches, so that | Luke 13: 18 He said therefore, "What is the kingdom of God like? And to what should I compare it? 19 It is like a mustard seed that someone took and sowed in the garden; it grew and became a tree, and the birds of the air made nests in its branches." |

nests in its branches."	the birds of the air can make nests in its shade."	

Some denominations in America take the concept of being 'born again,' very casually. Even those which take it seriously sometimes miss the implications. This parable makes it clear that even 'born again' Christians begin their new life as little children with only a seed of heaven in their hearts. While their new birth may be a gift from God (grace), with no requirement for 'works' on their part to receive it, they do not enter this new life as full-grown, mature Christians. Only with surrender and determination and practice can they grow into the mighty tree which attracts and shelters others.

Miscellaneous

Groom's attendants

| Matt. 9: 14 Then the disciples of John came to him, saying, "Why do we and the Pharisees fast often, but your disciples do not fast?" | Mark 2: 18 Now John's disciples and the Pharisees were fasting; and people came and said to him, "Why do John's disciples and the disciples of the Pharisees fast, but your disciples do not fast?" | Luke 5: 33 Then they said to him, "John's disciples, like the disciples of the Pharisees, frequently fast and pray, but your disciples eat and drink. |
| 15 And Jesus said to them, "The wedding guests cannot mourn as long as the bridegroom is with | 19 Jesus said to them, "The wedding guests cannot fast while the bridegroom is with them, can | 34 Jesus said to them, "You cannot make wedding guests fast while the bridegroom is with them, can you? |

them, can they?	they? As long as they have the bridegroom with them, they cannot fast.	
The days will come when the bridegroom is taken away from them, and then they will fast."	20 The days will come when the bridegroom is taken away from them, and then they will fast on that day."	35 The days will come when the bridegroom will be taken away from them, and then they will fast in those days."

Fasting is one obligation that most church members in overweight America find easiest to neglect. For Jesus, fasting was often an exercise in retreat from the world. In solitude he immersed himself in the Holy Spirit and recharged his spiritual batteries. In this age of omni-present television and I-pods and cell phones solitude is very difficult to experience and the virtues of solitude are virtually unknown by many church members. To forego any 'basic necessity' such as food for the sake of spiritual growth is equally difficult.

New cloth

| Matt. 9: 16 "No one sews a piece of unshrunk cloth on an old cloak, for the patch pulls away from the cloak, and a worse tear is made." | Mark 2: 21 "No one sews a piece of unshrunk cloth on an old cloak; otherwise, the patch pulls away from it, the new from the old, and a worse tear is made." | Luke 5: 36 He also told them a parable: "No one tears a piece from a new garment and sews it on an old garment; otherwise the new will be torn, and the piece from the new will not match the old." |

In this parable and the next, Jesus makes two points:

- Christianity cannot be grafted onto another religion, even Judaism;
- Newborn Christians must be completely changed and separated from what they were before their new birth.

New wine

| Matt. 9: 17 "Neither is new wine put into old wineskins; otherwise, the skins burst, and the wine is spilled, and the skins are destroyed; but new wine is put into fresh wineskins, and so both are preserved." | Mark 2: 22 "And no one puts new wine into old wineskins; otherwise, the wine will burst the skins, and the wine is lost, and so are the skins; but one puts new wine into fresh wineskins." | Luke 5: 37 "And no one puts new wine into old wineskins; otherwise the new wine will burst the skins and will be spilled, and the skins will be destroyed. 38 But new wine must be put into fresh wineskins." |

Here, Jesus observes that Jews will find it hard to accept the new wine which he offers.

It is equally hard for church members, raised on the teachings that glorify buildings and power and prestige and wealth, to accept the new wine the gospels present.

King's war plans

Luke 14: 31 "Or what king, going out to wage war against another king, will not sit down first and consider whether he is able with ten thousand to oppose the one who comes against him with twenty thousand?
32 If he cannot, then, while the other is still far away, he sends a

> delegation and asks for the terms of peace.
> 33 So therefore, none of you can become my disciple if you do not give up all your possessions."

Here, again, Jesus raises that awful possibility that our possessions will come between us and the creator god.

Salt without taste

| Matt. 5: 13 "You are the salt of the earth; but if salt has lost its taste, how can its saltiness be restored? It is no longer good for anything, but is thrown out and trampled under foot." | Mark 9: 50 "Salt is good; but if salt has lost its saltiness, how can you season it? Have salt in yourselves, and be at peace with one another." | Luke 14: 34 "Salt is good; but if salt has lost its taste, how can its saltiness be restored?" |

Jesus calls his followers the salt of the earth and cautions them against letting their faith and teachings become polluted or corrupt lest they be 'thrown out.' Again, he warns that salvation can be lost if the individual's faith and practice become corrupted.

Afterword

If you've read this far, you can guess what comes next: the questions 1) How much of this can I believe? and 2) What am I going to do about it?

I'm not a professional football player, but I can tell the difference between a field goal and a fumble. I'm not a professional farmer, but I can distinguish between a fig and a thorn. And, I'm not a professional religionist, but I can tell that helping fix a church dinner is not the same as working miracles of healing or even feeding the poor. If I can make these distinctions, then surely you can too. Of course, your spiritual leaders can, too.

The fact that you and I may not be able to work miracles doesn't mean it couldn't happen. And it doesn't excuse us from serving the creator god in every way we can.

So, I invite you to consider:

1) If my prophecy is false, then Jesus wasn't serious when he promised miracle powers to believers. (Of course, he may also have been kidding when he promised eternal life to followers.) He was probably kidding when he told followers to worship him instead of wealth and to pray for their enemies. And especially when he told them to turn the other cheek. If my prophecy is false, then I will go to Hell along with a few who have believed me. (If there is a Hell.) If my prophecy is false, then God will truly help those who help themselves. And greed will be good.

2) If, on the other hand, my prophecy is true, then millions of well-intentioned people who worship the comfort and opulence of 'the church;' those who ignore the gospel lessons; or those who worship the

promises of Prosperity Theology and neglect the poor; will go to Hell along with millions of others who have worshipped Mammon through the ages.

3) A decision to regard this prophecy as 'interesting' or 'heretical' may condemn you to continue ignoring the gospel teachings. You could rise up in outrage and vilify the book. You could determine to 'decide later.'

Or you could decide to seriously consider changing your expectations and your life. **Even Jesus will not force you to follow him.**

The passages I included in this book are not the only teachings in the gospels. But, if you can't or won't apply these teachings, why think you will apply the others? The teachings of Jesus are the narrow gate[16] through which we draw closer to the creator god. As you focus on doing the positive things he commands, your ability to do God's will will grow stronger. As you affirm your faith and surrender, those qualities will increase. As you accept God's love and provisions for your life, they will become a more powerful part of your life.

Perhaps the last question is "Why bother?" If you can't trust Jesus to keep his promises about working miracles; if you can't trust God's promise to provide for your daily needs; then how can you trust God's promises about salvation? Why pretend? Why try?

Millions of people don't even pretend to believe in Jesus and his saving mission. Millions haven't even heard of him. Others look at the self-centered church and its self-righteous members and reject Jesus outright. Millions of others go to church and pretend to believe him while ignoring his commands.

I encourage you to reread this book and the gospels with an eye to the changes they call you to make in your thinking and in your behavior.

Your decisions will determine your fate.

---

[16] Matt. 7: 13-14.

Appendix I

'Believing in' vs. 'Believing'

N.B. <u>Satan's greatest lie</u> is the introduction of the concept of 'believing in' Jesus rather than 'believing' Jesus. To 'believe in' Jesus is little more than an intellectual exercise for many, just as believing in Napoleon or Hitler, or corrupt politicians as historical characters, is an intellectual exercise. Believing the words of Jesus and acting on that belief is much more demanding and powerful. 'Believing in' Jesus without believing his teachings and acting on them is probably worse than worthless.

Most church members say they believe in the concept of Jesus as the Son of God. But we should keep in mind that even the devil and the demons 'believe in' Jesus as the Son of God. And the scribes and Pharisees and priests 'believed in' Jesus on the night of his arrest. Satan surely doesn't care whether you 'believe in' Jesus so long as you don't believe Jesus.

(The Heretic's Handbook pp. 45-46.)

Appendix II

God's Will

God's will is not only something God imposes on the world. It is also what man does in response to Jesus' teachings and in obedience to God. It may be difficult or impossible to know what God wants in specific situations, but the Bible gives us plenty of insights into God's will in general. Just drawing on the teachings and examples of Jesus we can know that God wants men:

- To love him more than possessions or other people or other gods
- To love their neighbors as themselves
- To receive the salvation he has made available to them through Jesus Christ
- To share the good news of his love with other men
- To love their enemies and pray for them
- To turn the other cheek
- To put their trust in him and be dependent on him
- To be totally surrendered to his purpose for them
- To demonstrate their faith by performing works (miracles) of healing
- To demonstrate his faithfulness to those who believe him
- To share their possessions with the less fortunate
- To suffer criticism or die willingly to spread the faith

If you're not doing God's will then you may not be a member of Christ's body. And you may not have any claim on God's answers to your prayers or on eternal life. Nothing contributes more to your Christian growth than doing God's will. And God's will can serve as a beacon in guiding your everyday life.

(The Heretic's Handbook pp. 77-78.)